Baseball Puzzlers

YOU MAKE THE CALL

Wayne Stewart

Illustrated by
Sandy Hoffman

Sterling Publishing Co., Inc.
New York

*To the best one-two-three lineup around:
my wife Nancy
and our two sons, Sean and Scott*

Edited by Claire Bazinet

Library of Congress Cataloging-in-Publication Data
Stewart, Wayne, 1951–
    Baseball puzzlers: you make the call / by Wayne Stewart;
illustrated by Sandy Hoffman.
        p. cm.
    Includes index.
    ISBN 0-8069-2691-0
    1. Baseball–Miscellanea. 2. Questions and answers. I. Title.
GV867.3 .S85 2000
796.357–dc21   00-028501

10 9 8 7 6 5 4 3 2 1

First paperback edition published in 2001 by
Sterling Publishing Company, Inc.
387 Park Avenue South, New York, N.Y. 10016
© 2000 by Wayne Stewart
Distributed in Canada by Sterling Publishing
ᶜ/o Canadian Manda Group, One Atlantic Avenue,
Suite 105, Toronto, Ontario, Canada M6K 3E7
Distributed in Great Britain and Europe by Chris Lloyd at Orca Book
Services, Stanley House, Fleets Lane, Poole BH15 3AJ, England.
Distributed in Australia by Capricorn Link (Australia) Pty. Ltd.
P.O. Box 704, Windsor, NSW 2756 Australia
Manufactured in the United States of America
All rights reserved

Sterling ISBN 0-8069-2691-0 Trade
                 0-8069-2696-1 Paper

Contents

Part 1

YOU'RE THE MANAGER

Let's start by allowing you to sit in the dugout and make managerial decisions based on real-life big-league situations. Armed with the information provided, you must make the call(s). If you're good at it, you might even earn the kind of praise that legends like Leo Durocher gained. Phil Regan felt Leo "The Lip" was a good manager because "He was always an inning ahead of everybody else. He didn't go against the book very much; he was just good."

Chapter One

OFFENSIVE STRATEGIES

This first chapter is based exclusively on offensive moves. Test yourself to see if *you* can be an inning ahead of everybody else, so to speak. Good luck.

Switch away from Switch-Hitting?

Being a switch-hitter gives a batter an advantage over those who hit only one way. Do you suppose, however, there is ever a time when a manager would ask a player to quit switch-hitting?

Answer: Not often, but this does happen. First of all, most managers don't like it when one of their pitchers switch-hits. The reason for this is simple. Say a right-handed pitcher also hits righty, which is normal for most of the population. In such a case, his precious pitching arm is not exposed to the ball as it travels to him in the batter's box. That arm is closer to the umpire, protected from the pitch by the batter's body.

But, when that person turns around to switch-hit, in this case now batting left handed, his pitching arm is the one that could get hit by a pitch. Why take a chance on such an occurrence, is the logic of managers. Besides, why worry about switch-hitting, when it's a pitcher's job to pitch, not to belt the ball.

Still, some famous pitchers did insist on switch-hitting. That certainly must include Early Wynn (although he threw and hit righty exclusively for four of the 23 years he spent in the majors). Wynn not only won 300 games, he hit .214, drilled 17 homers, and was even used as pinch hitter 90 times.

Ted Lyons, like Wynn, a Hall-of-Famer, pitched for 21 seasons, hitting a robust .233 from both sides of the plate. And, in one of the oddest situations ever, Tony Mullane, who could throw the ball with either arm—and actually did so in several games—was a switch-hitter (.243 lifetime overall) for 12 of his 13 years in the "bigs."

Yet another member of the Hall of Fame, Mordecai "Three Finger" Brown, hit over .200 as a switch-hitter over 14 years. Coincidentally, his lifetime E.R.A. of 2.06 has the same numerals as his career batting average, .206!

Then there was Hank Johnson, who hit .215 lifetime. In 1933, his only year of switch-hitting, he hit 16 points higher than his career average, yet didn't return to switch-hitting during the last four years of his career.

Mickey Lolich, who won 25 games in 1971, hit both ways in all but three of his 16 years in the big leagues (but hit only .110). A contemporary of Lolich is the answer to a tricky trivia question: Name the last switch-hitter to win the American League M.V.P. The obvious guess is Mickey Mantle, but the actual answer is pitcher Vida Blue in 1971, the same year he won the Cy Young Award. Interestingly, another pretty good hitter, Rick Sutcliffe, threw right handed, but hit lefty (.181 career).

Enough of pitchers; there's another reason to discourage a player from switch-hitting—it "ain't workin'!" In late August of 1999, Todd Hundley was struggling as a two-way hitter. At the time, all 19 of his home runs came while he was hitting lefty, and his batting average as a righty was a dismal .098. Clearly it was time to quit hitting right handed. He said he'd stick with batting lefty as long as it felt comfortable, maybe even indefinitely.

One other recent example of a man who abandoned switch-hitting is J.T. Snow. He broke into the majors in 1992. In 1998 he hit .248, his lowest average for a full season since his rookie year. So, in 1999 he gave up hitting right handed, where his numbers were poor. Actually, he gave it up during the last week of the 1998 season due to injuries. The move made sense since he had, in fact, hit a mere .189 as a righty from 1996 to 1998. He wound up hitting .274 in '99 with 24 HR and 98 RBI, nine homers and 19 RBI better than the previous season.

Run on Them?

Say your team has some pretty decent base-stealers. One factor in deciding whether or not you want your runners on the go is who's on the mound. If a pitcher isn't strong at holding runners on, it becomes time for giving your runners the good old green light. Test your knowledge on the following six pitchers and their ability to keep a runner honest at first base.

Chuck Finley   Greg Maddux   Dwight Gooden
Andy Pettitte   Sterling Hitchcock   Bret Saberhagen

Answers: Finley is easy to run on. Although he's a southpaw, and that is supposed to be a plus in holding runners on, Finley's high leg kick hurts him.

Maddux, too, is easy to run against. Despite his outstanding ability as a pitcher, including his fine defense, he has difficulty holding men on base.

The same holds true for Gooden. Even when he was a great pitcher during his early days with the New York Mets, he had a single glaring flaw. Runners took liberties with him; the only difficulty the offense had back then was reaching base in the first place against the young, sensational Gooden.

Pettitte is extremely difficult to steal on. Experts agree almost unanimously that this lefty has the best move to first in all of baseball although (or because) he frequently flirts with the balk rule. He loves to throw over to keep runners tight to the bag. In 1998, for example, only four pitchers threw to first more often than Pettitte.

Meanwhile, Hitchcock, who has a good move, is nevertheless rather easy to run on. Like Finley, Hitchcock's big kick allows runners to get a good jump. Considering he's a left-hander, many base-burglars succeed against him. In fact, in 1998 only a small handful of lefties had a worse success rate of stolen bases against them.

Finally, Saberhagen. He's one of the best right-handed pitchers in the game when it comes to thwarting base-stealers. His move is quick and that, of course, helps a great deal. Don't run on him.

More on Saberhagen

Against some pitchers, a batter might take the first pitch just to see what the pitcher looks like. Also, at times when a pitcher first enters the game, the other team might take a look, wait him out, see if he can throw strikes. Would it be a good idea to do this against Saberhagen, or does he throw strikes so reliably you'd just be wasting a pitch, getting behind in the count for nothing?

Answer: His control is outstanding. In 1994 when he was with the New York Mets, he struck out 143 batters in 177⅓ innings. Over that span he walked a ridiculously low 13 batters. That means you'd have a long wait between walks—he'd go nearly 14 innings between surrendering a free pass. That same year, he actually had more victories than walks given up (14 to 13), and he came close to doing that again in 1999 with 11 walks against 10 victories. By August of 1999, he had gone 10 of 17 starts without issuing a single walk. Infielder Mike Bordick said, "His control is great, his walks are real low. He's one of those guys who's going to come at you."

Take a Strike?

There's a difference between taking a pitch, usually with a count of 3-and-0, and taking a strike. At the lower levels of baseball, if your team is losing late in the game and you are desperate to start a rally (especially against a pitcher who might be tiring and/or getting wild), you might instruct your batters not to swing at a pitch until the pitcher proves he can throw a strike. In other words, the batter is taking each and every pitch until there is a strike on him. Do major leaguers do this, too?

Reality: Yes, they do. Just listen to former Detroit Tiger star shortstop Alan Trammell. "Certainly there are times to do this. I played for Sparky Anderson for 17 years, and it was mandatory in the eighth and ninth inning, if you were trailing, to take a strike." He continued, "There were a few exceptions: a guy like Dennis Eckersley who, of course, would come in there and get strike one on you all the time. So you didn't want to give him one.

"But most of my career playing for Sparky, we'd take a strike. That's the 'old-school' way. That has changed somewhat depending on who's pitching nowadays, but, yes, you do take a strike."

Minor league manager Paul Carey (with Savannah of Class A in 1999) said he teaches his players the same thing. "It's an important strategy when you're down late in the game if the pitcher isn't throwing strikes."

Mike Bordick added, "Late in the game, especially when an established closer is in the game and his role is to get ahead, you don't do it." He cited examples such as John Wetteland and Mariano Rivera. Bordick says taking a strike is not as common as it was in the days of Sparky Anderson, even against starters who are still in the game during late innings. "Unless they've shown that they're going to tire in the end, they're going to want to get ahead," he said, so they will try to throw a first-pitch strike.

Take a Strike versus Pedro Martinez?

It's late in the game and you're facing the outstanding right-hander, Pedro Martinez. Is he the kind of guy you take a strike against, or would that be a bad move?

Answer: In 1999, Cleveland's infield and first-base coach, Brian Graham, commented, "The game situation dictates your approach offensively. With some pitchers, even if Pedro Martinez is late into a game, you want to get a pitch you can hit. Because if he gets ahead of you, he has such an array of pitches that you're in trouble. So, you better get a pitch to hit, and if it happens to be the first pitch, you better take your shot at the first pitch. He's got a lot better chance of nibbling once he gets ahead of you in that situation."

Just to give a sampling of other pitchers and other situations, Graham tossed in, "If it's Roberto Hernandez, you take a strike because you never know if he's going to be right around the plate all the time. You definitely take a strike on Jose Mesa because his out pitch is the fastball and his get-ahead pitch is the fastball. So he's got to get it over the plate, so you're still going to get a chance at the fastball later in the count. It depends on who the pitcher is and who's hitting behind you, too. If you're down at the end of the order and you have a guy who's not going to hit a home run, then it's a tough call," he concluded.

Are You Orthodox or Unorthodox?

Here's a strategy that is quite unorthodox—would you consider doing it? You've got a good bat-handler at the plate, but he's got two strikes on him. Under those circumstances, would you put on the suicide squeeze play?

Answer: You probably shouldn't; it's a very risky play. The brazen Don Zimmer called for that play when he managed the Chicago Cubs. His bat magician was Ryne Sandberg. Zimmer had so much confidence in his stellar second baseman, he felt the play could work.

By the way, Zimmer also had the Cubs' Vance Law (and a few other players during his managerial years) hit and run with the bases loaded.

Chapter Two

DEFENSIVE STRATEGIES

Now it's your turn to make decisions based on the defensive side of the game. Again, pretend you're a major league manager and see what you'd do when faced with many defensive dilemmas. In some cases, your knowledge of players and the game will be tested in quiz form. In any event, good luck. Incidentally, for this book, when a player's age is mentioned, it refers to his age at the start of the 2000 season.

Bullpen Decision

Mike Hargrove was faced with two of the most important decisions of his career back in Game 5 of the 1995 American League Championship Series. The Series was tied at two apiece, with Cleveland up against the potent Seattle Mariners. The Indians encountered a dangerous seventh inning situation as runners were on the corners and Ken Griffey, Jr., a left-handed hitter, was at the plate with one out; a mere long-fly ball would tie the contest. At that point, Hargrove brought in a lefty, Paul Assenmacher. The Indians relief pitcher did his job, fanning Griffey. Hargrove's first decision had paid off.

Now, the next hitter was a powerful righty, Jay Buhner. Hargrove's second decision (and now your dilemma) was this: should you allow Assenmacher to face Buhner? If not, would you bring in middle-innings relief pitcher Eric Plunk or go straight to your big gun, closer Jose Mesa with his darting fastball?

Remember, it's late in the game and you're trying to hold tenaciously to a 3–2 lead. Remember, too, the day before this game Buhner had hit a three-run shot off Plunk to win a 5–2, 11-inning nail-biter. If you lose this one, Seattle takes the upper hand in this fight for the pennant.

13

Assenmacher later said, "It was a big game. We needed to win it; we didn't need to go into Seattle down three games to two. Then they could've rested Randy Johnson an extra day."

What happened? Common baseball strategy, also known as playing it by the book, dictated Hargrove bring in his right-handed set-up pitcher Plunk at that point (so, if that's your answer, you made a "book" decision). In reality, the manager stuck with Assenmacher. "I just liked the way that Paul was throwing," explained Hargrove. "I felt that the way we were going to try to pitch Buhner [was something that] Paul could attack better than anybody else we had to bring in."

In fact, Assenmacher said that, after retiring Griffey, he never once looked towards the bench expecting to see Hargrove pop out of the dugout to lift him. "You can't have that type of mind set when you're pitching. You take it one hitter at a time. After I got Griffey, I believe we had a discussion about Buhner, but there were two outs so now a flyball or a groundball wasn't going to be able to score [a run], he needed to get a hit. I felt I had good enough stuff at that time to get him out."

He wasn't the only one with a good feeling about the move to keep him on the mound. Hargrove said, "It's one of those things that just felt right." Many veteran managers contend you simply have to make some decisions along those bold lines.

Hargrove readily knew if the move backfired, the media and fans alike would have vilified him. "That's what they hire you for. I mean, you can cover your butt all day long and it may not do any good. There are times you have to go out and have the courage of your convictions." Still, it always helps when you have success.

Assenmacher relived that day, saying, "After I got Griffey out, I was in a situation where I could pitch around Buhner if I needed to face Tino [Martinez], but it was just one of those things where I just felt I had a good curveball going that day to him. Even though the one I threw him and struck him out was a little bit up, it broke sharp at the end."

Both Hargrove and Assenmacher were aware of other factors, too. For example, as the veteran reliever said, "It was a case where if I walked him, so what? Tino [a lefty] was coming up next, but once I got the two strikes, I figured I might as well go after him, try to finish him off."

Defensive Decision #1

Let's say Ryan Klesko, or any such pull hitter, is at the plate. Your pitcher is not overpowering; let's say, in fact, he throws quite a bit of off-speed stuff. How would you play your infield defensively?

Answer: What many managers do in such a situation is put on an infield shift. Sometimes it can be so exaggerated the third baseman plays where the shortstop normally would be on a lefty hitter such as Klesko. The shortstop, meantime, is usually standing slightly to either the right or left of the second base bag. So, at times three defensive players are on the right side of the infield to many dead pull hitters.

Defensive Decision #2

There is one out when a batter smacks a routine single to right field. The runner off first base possesses average to slightly above-average speed. The game is tied and in the late innings. The runner is determined to streak all the way to third base because if he makes it, he can score on, for example, a sacrifice fly (or a wild pitch, or a passed ball, for that matter). At any rate, if you were able to have Jose Guillen in right, would you feel you had a defensive advantage over the other team?

Answer: Yes. The runner would probably be gunned down as Guillen, like a handful of other fine right fielders, can throw a rope from just about any distance in the outfield.

The Pirates were unhappy with Guillen in 1999 at times. Still, despite the fact that they sent him back to the minor leagues twice, and eventually traded him to the Tampa Bay

Devil Rays, Pittsburghers immediately recognized that Guillen has a Roberto Clemente-like arm. One general manager called the Tampa trade a steal, saying Guillen is much desired by many G.M.'s. At the age of 23, look for him to pile up a bunch of assists before he quits.

Only a few other men can throw like Guillen. Before undergoing surgery, Jay Buhner was known for his fine arm. In fact, Harold Baines said, "He has a great arm." One American League coach added, "He is very accurate, never misses a cut-off, the ball's always low, and he makes very few mistakes, he never throws to the wrong base." B.J. Surhoff agreed, saying, "Jay's arm is obviously very respected—strong and accurate."

Still, Guillen is perhaps better. Alex Ochoa said, "He has a great arm." He even compared Guillen's gun to that of Vladimir Guerrero (who was called by one national publication a "future M.V.P."). "It's tough to call that one," said Ochoa, concerning the Guillen–Guerrero debate. "They've both got great arms. It's tough to choose who's better."

When it comes, for example, to stopping runners from going first-to-third on a base hit to right, Ochoa says you're not going to run on either man. He added, "If they get a ball and they get to it quickly, they stop you [on the base paths] automatically. Both of them do a good job in getting to the ball and letting go of it quickly."

Defensive Decision #3

You are Frank Thomas's manager. He comes to your office one day and says, "Skipper, I feel I hit better when I'm playing first base more so than when I'm the designated hitter. How about it?" Would you allow him to play the field?

Answer: This time it's your call, and yours alone. You might permit him to have his way, as it's wise to keep superstars happy. However, in truth, he is a defensive liability. At 6' 5" and about 270 pounds he has limited range, and his hands aren't exactly soft and supple. He even admitted he's no Gold Glover, saying he wishes he could play defense like Mark Grace. He considers Grace a first baseman who plays like a shortstop. Clearly, then, most managers would prefer Thomas make his living with the bat as the D.H.

However, it should be noted that in 1999, Chicago White Sox manager Jerry Manuel felt otherwise. In August Thomas complained that he did not want to play in the field. He said, "I've had my time in the field. I know the position I should be playing and that's D.H. I feel good D.H.ing, more comfortable." Manuel's argument was Thomas actually has better offensive numbers when he plays first than when he's used as the D.H. At the time of that comment, Thomas was a .346 hitter while playing the field versus his .286 average as the D.H. From 1996 through 1998 he hit .352 while at first and .274 as the D.H.

His final games played totals for 1999 show that he played first base 49 times and was the D.H. on 82 occasions. He hit for a .305 average (his second lowest ever) to go with his disappointing totals of 15 homers and 77 runs driven in—both representing career lows.

Defensive Decision #4

It's late in the game and you want to preserve your lead. Although you didn't start Darren Lewis in the outfield, you could certainly put him out there now. Would you consider using him as your late-inning defensive replacement for an outfielder of average ability?

Answer: You'd be wise to insert Lewis. As of 1999 he was the record holder for the most consecutive errorless games played and the most outfield chances accepted without committing an error. Those records cover a flawless period of 392 games and 938 total chances.

Defensive Decision #5

Late in the game, you're nursing a one-run lead. The opponents are at the plate. If the batter should put the ball right down the third-base line, it's a sure double. Many managers will protect the line by having their third baseman hug the foul line, playing very near to it. A few strategists have said that over the course of a season this move will give up too many more singles through the left side of the diamond than the normal defensive deployment. They contend that tons of singles eventually will hurt more than the occasional double down the line that you deny. How would you play this?

Giving his major league opinion, Phil Garner stated, "In most all of the cases, we'll guard the line in the seventh inning on, and you're playing for the one time that the ball goes down the line. You don't want the double. If you give up the single, they still have to get him over. They still have to, say, keep from having a double play. So, you're playing against the unusual. You're not playing the odds there, you're playing the other side of the odds. I'd much rather them have a single and then we'll take a shot on getting a double play, rather than let them have a double, bunt him over, and then it's easy to get him in.

"It's like an insurance policy; you hope you don't need it, but you want to have it there in case you do," he commented.

Any Exceptions?

There are exceptions. Garner demonstrated how a thinking manager is always flexible and at times is even willing to go against his own usual style of play. "We didn't guard the line against Kansas City [in July of 1999] because we felt like one of the players that they had, we couldn't throw him out anyway. We felt this guy can steal the base at will. If he singles, he's going to get a 'double' anyway. So, why guard against a double—he'll be at second anyway."

Incidentally, to show you how shrewd managers are, when asked who the Kansas City player was, Garner replied with a sly chuckle, "I'm not going to say that because we play them again and I don't want them to know what we're thinking about." Unfortunately, the managerial game being what it is, he didn't get a rematch with the Royals as he was fired by the Brewers on August 11th after being at the helm for nearly eight years.

When it comes to outfield defense, is there a strategy concerning giving away singles while preventing doubles? If so, what's the thinking here?

Answer: Garner expounded once more, "Same philosophy, we'll play our outfielders back." With a deep outfield configuration, singles may fall in front of the defense, but the gaps are easier to plug, thus cutting off potential doubles. "Make them score from first, rather than giving them the double," said Garner. Anyone can see, it's clearly a whole lot easier to score from second than from first.

Good Question, but No Correct Answer

This time you get a question for which there is no answer. Still, consider the dilemma. Since it could be argued that pitching is the one most important element of a team's defense, this question is vital. If you had to win one big game, say, to win the division title or even to clinch the World Series, who would you want on the mound?

One could make a claim for quite a few fine pitchers. For example, it might be tempting to go with the only man who has won the Cy Young Award five times, Roger Clemens. He's proven he can dominate a game—having struck out a single-game (nine innings) record 20 batters not once, but twice.

Severe, and perhaps unfair, critics might argue that Clemens doesn't win the big post-season games. Going into 1999, his record in nine such contests was a meager 1–2. When he won his first post-season start on October 5, 1999, it marked his first post-season win since 1986. However, in his next post-season start 11 days later, he was rocked. Not only did he lose the game, his pitching line read: 2 innings pitched, 6 hits, for 5 earned runs giving him an E.R.A for that day of 22.50! Furthermore, he actually held four negative pitching records for American League Championship Series play. One of those records was for the seven earned runs he gave up on October 7, 1986.

In 1999, the Yankees finished off a streak of winning 18 of 19 post-season games when they swept the Series. The only loss during that incredible 19-game span belonged to Clemens when he was tagged hard by the Red Sox.

Finally, though, he enjoyed satisfaction when, at the age of 37, he clinched that final game of the 1999 World Series, gaining his first ever Series ring while evening his lifetime post-season record at 3–3.

Then there's Greg Maddux with his four Cy Young Awards. No pitcher won more than his 176 games during the 1990's. Believe it or not, though, his post-season slate isn't exactly stellar, either. From 1995 to 1998 he went 1–0 in each opening round of post-season play (in the Division Series). However, his National League Championship Series record was sub-.500 at 3–6 (a .333 win-loss percentage). Finally, in the World Series prior to 1999, he was just a .500 pitcher at 2–2 although, to be honest, his E.R.A. for those four contests was a dazzling 1.99. And, in his first three 1999 post-season starts he went 1–1 with a no decision in a strong outing. Finally, his 1999 Series loss dropped him to a lifetime slate of 10–10 in "prime-time" play.

Similarly, the case of Randy Johnson is perplexing. He won his first two post-season games back in 1995, but from then through his first post-season start in 1999, he went 0–6 (including an 0–5 ledger in his first-round starts). His 0–6 skid established a new futility record. All that from the man who, in 1999, recorded the fourth highest strikeout total in the annals of the game, 364.

The point here is not to bash Clemens, Maddux, and Johnson (you could even toss in Cy Young winner Tom Glavine, now 10–11 in lifetime post-season play)—all proven stars—but rather to show how difficult such a decision would be. That's why winning managers get paid pretty well. It's also why after they make a few too many wrong decisions they get fired. So, good luck in picking your starter.

After seeing Orlando Hernandez excel lately in post-season play (3–0 overall in 1999), you might be tempted to give him the ball in big games. He entered the 1999 Series with a post-season record of 4–0 with the fifth best E.R.A. ever of 0.97 in five post-season starts. Then he won yet another game, capturing the first contest of the World Series.

Too bad 1999 Series MVP Mariano Rivera isn't a starter—his post-season E.R.A., based on two earned runs over 47⅓ innings, is a nearly invisible 0.36! That's the lowest for any pitcher ever with 30 or more post-season innings pitched. He ended the 1999 season with a streak of 25 2/3 consecutive shutout innings pitched in post-season play. Not bad for a 29-year-old guy who grew up playing with gloves cut out of cardboard back in his native land of Panama.

Time Machine

Incidentally, if you could pick a pitcher from the past, you might want to think about giving the ball to Sandy Koufax. Hall of Fame manager Tommy Lasorda said the great southpaw is the very man he'd go to when desperate for a big win. No wonder—Koufax, also a Hall of Fame resident, sported a scintillating Series E.R.A. of 0.95.

Other wise selections would include Whitey Ford, author of the most World Series wins (10), or Babe Ruth with an unbelievable Series E.R.A. of 0.87 (#3 all-time) to go with his perfect 3–0 win-loss total, good for a 1.000 win-loss percentage (tied #1 all-time). How about Bob Gibson? His win total of seven is the second best ever, as are his 92 strike-outs, only two less than Ford who pitched in 22 games to nine for Gibson. Finally, you might consider Lefty Gomez, who was perfect in Series play with the best ever win-loss mark of 6–0.

Who Would You Take Out?

Some outfielders are so good, you simply wouldn't replace them late in the game. Although injured for much of 1999, Jim Edmonds is the subject of this question: When healthy, would you consider him one of the outfielders too good to substitute for, or is he the type you'd bench in a split second?

Answer: Edmonds won Gold Gloves in 1997 and 1998, gaining fame for his numerous highlight film catches. The best of his many great grabs, and, in fact, perhaps the greatest catch ever made in center field (including the Willie Mays catch in the 1954 Series) came in 1997.

Like Mays, Edmonds had to take off at the crack of the bat, spin, race directly away from home plate, and haul in the ball on the dead run. What made the Edmonds catch even more spectacular was the fact that he caught the ball over his shoulder with his back to the plate as he dove at the last second towards the centerfield fence. If you've seen the catch

you know how amazing it was. If you haven't seen it, forget it—you can't even begin to imagine it!

The fact that he doesn't exactly have great speed made that play (and many of his other plays) even more impressive. He gets great jumps and he plays the hitters very well. No, you would hardly want to substitute for him.

When Is the Right Moment for the Hidden Ball Trick?

Are there certain moments when it's most propitious to try the hidden ball trick? In this case consider the runner and the game situation as you grope for the answer.

Answer: Matt Williams is adept at this play, and he seems to pick on players who don't have a great deal of major league experience. Over the last few seasons he tried this play on a rookie, Jed Hensen—it worked—and Neifi Perez back when he was still a fledgling—it would have worked, but the pitcher violated a rule during the play and that resulted in a balk and negated the sleight-of-hand trick.

You want to save trick plays for the right game situation too. Why waste this trick on a lopsided game? Instead, save it for perhaps a tight game or when you're in a tough spot—when you really need an out.

Then, too, first baseman Sean Berry says it won't work unless another factor is involved. "Usually, there's some sort of distraction that helps set up the hidden ball trick. A guy's taking off his ankle pad, not paying attention, and the opposing bench isn't paying attention.

"Maybe the pitcher, who's not allowed on the mound without the ball [in this situation], might walk around acting like he's struggling [to distract the opponents]," said Berry.

In 1999 J.T. Snow of the San Francisco Giants victimized the Los Angeles Dodgers. Carlos Perez, their starting pitcher, beat out a throw to first for a single. In typical Perez fashion, he celebrated his hit as he returned from hustling through the bag and down the right field line a few yards.

Snow then indicated to his pitcher that the play was on as Perez seemed oblivious of everything but his self-satisfied gestures. Sure enough, it worked. Snow later said he felt sneaky and nervous as he waited for Perez to step off the bag. And, then, gotcha!

Berry observed that, against Perez, it was a perfect situation, as the pitcher had just given up a hit to the opposing pitcher. Maybe preying upon a pitcher who isn't experienced on the base paths made sense as well.

Do Big Leaguers Believe in Payback?

Did Snow perhaps pick Perez as his victim to teach him a lesson about showing other players up? Was this a pickoff with some retribution? Tony Muser, manager of the 1999 Kansas City Royals said, "I think that happens in baseball, you 'identify' yourself. When players do things on the field with antics, they draw attention to themselves. And what Perez did is draw attention to himself, and there is what you call subtle intimidation in this game, or payback. No doubt about it.

"'I don't like what you do on the mound, so you better be alert because I'm going to get you.' And that's exactly what happens.

"It's not that it's a matter of who's good or bad, it's competitiveness, and players do compete. They watch body language, they read statements in papers, and they listen to interviews. Players today are the most informed baseball people in the world—they know what's going on," Muser concluded. Unfortunately for Perez, he didn't know what was going on and Snow made him pay the price.

Phil Garner disagrees about the revenge factor. "You just figure, if a guy's out there celebrating, he's not paying attention to what he's doing on the field, so you take a chance on a guy like that. When you get a guy who doesn't appear like he's in the game, those are the guys you try to make it work on."

Use a Decoy?

How is it possible for a manager to use a relief pitcher as a decoy to gain an advantage over the other manager?

Answer: Jesse Orosco explained this one: "I've been used as a decoy a lot of times so the other team won't bring up a left-hander to the plate. I may not even be throwing hard [in the bullpen], but just for them to see a reliever warming up [can work]."

He said that while the other team can't take a chance that he's just a decoy, the reliever himself will know. "They'll just say, 'Use your own judgment [on how hard to warm up], you're probably not going to be in the game.'

"It happens every once in a while. I did it a number of times for Davey Johnson [in Baltimore]. As a manager, you have to have some tricks up your sleeve," he stated.

You Rate Them

Now is your chance to rate some more players defensively. We'll give you a player noted for his offense, and you must rank him as being either great, good, fair, below average, or poor based upon his glove work.

Jeff Bagwell   Kenny Lofton   Gary Sheffield
Tony Gwynn   Rickey Henderson

Compare them now to our evaluations: "Bags" is a stand-out at first base. Fellow first baseman Sean Berry praised the somewhat overlooked Bagwell. "I like how he plays," said Berry, "very aggressive. I try to watch him a lot."

As for Lofton, overall you must give him a stong grade. With his absolutely blazing speed, he is capable of running down almost any ball hit to the outfield. In 1988, he was the sixth man on the University of Arizona's basketball team that made it to the Final Four in NCAA play. The next year he played the starting point guard position, and at one point helped lead them to a number-one ranking in the polls.

He still has great leaping skills and has robbed many a player of what should have been a home run. One negative note on Lofton, a four-time Gold Glove winner, is his arm. It is a bit weak, he has a tendency to sometimes throw off target a bit, and he misses his cutoff man too much.

Next, Sheffield. He was once considered to be below average in the outfield. Now he's average to perhaps a bit above average with a good arm and fine speed.

Gwynn, at 39, is a below average outfielder. He doesn't get to a lot of balls that most right fielders reach, and his arm is a bit on the weak side.

Henderson was a fine left fielder in his prime. In fact, Hall of Fame left fielder Billy Williams said he is one of the best ever at that position. Nevertheless, at the age of 41, he has declined a bit—call him average now. He's still fast, and that can help overcome mistakes, but his arm is not that great, so opponents will run on him.

How to Play Them

If you had a chance to glance at the charts teams keep showing where each batter hits each ball that he puts into play for each season, you'd have a pretty good idea where to play those batters. Without benefit of such charts, test your knowledge of the following men by stating where you'd play them defensively. Would you play them to hit the ball to the opposite field, or to pull the ball, or to spray it?

Garret Anderson   Mark McGwire   Troy Glaus
Nomar Garciaparra   Derek Jeter

Answers: Anderson pretty much fits the definition of a spray hitter, making him fairly hard to defend. He uses all fields and did particularly well in 1998, hitting .294; in 1999 he raised his average to .303. Basically you might place your fielders straight away, neither playing him to pull or to go the other way.

McGwire. Easy one. This guys pulls virtually everything; that means he fits the bill as a "dead pull hitter." Of his historic 70 home runs in 1998, only three went to right or right-center field. No man hit more homers in the 1990s than McGwire (405 HR), and probably no man pulled as many homers, either.

Glaus is the man who actually broke McGwire's home run record. Well, the Pac-10 Conference collegiate record, that is. Glaus, a U.C.L.A. star is, like Big Mac, a pull hitter.

As for Garciaparra, despite his power he is a spray hitter in that he can hit the ball virtually anywhere, and do so with power. Some spray hitters are weak, Punch-and-Judy hitters; Garciaparra hits with authority.

Jeter is such a good hitter he can hit it anywhere. If you throw him inside, his bat is so quick he can inside-out the ball to the opposite field. In 1998, against lefties, almost every groundball he hit went to (or through) the left side, as he'd pull the ball often.

Chapter Three

1999 MANAGERIAL CALLS

For this chapter every scenario is one that happened during the 1999 season. So, you get to make the calls based on recent real-life situations, allowing you to pit your skills against current big league managers.

Pitch to Him? Free Pass?

On July 16th the Detroit Tigers faced the Houston Astros during an interleague contest. There were two outs in the ninth inning of a tie game. Houston had a runner at second base with a tough hitter at the plate, All Star Craig Biggio. Biggio was coming off a .325 season in 1998 and was a career .292 hitter.

The on-deck hitter, on the other hand, was reserve player Russ Johnson, who had only 13 major league at-bats for the entire 1998 season (.231 that year). Also, Johnson, at the time, was sporting a soft .224 average for 1999. Additionally, all of the Astros pinch hitters had been used up. The pitcher on the hill for Detroit was Doug Brocail, a journeyman.

Basically, that's all the information you need to know. What do you suppose Tigers manager Larry Parrish did? What would you do?

Answer: This is almost certainly one time when the average fan could out-manage the professional. This situation cries out for an intentional walk to Biggio. In reality, Parrish decided to go right at Biggio; the move failed miserably. Biggio drilled a single and the Astros won the game, 2–1.

Even Parrish knew he had made a huge mistake. He said, "I screwed that up. There's no way that I should let that guy beat you. No way. That's a situation where I've got to walk him." Even big leaguers sometimes second-guess themselves.

Walk This Guy?

On August 15, 1999, the Baltimore Orioles were playing the Cleveland Indians, trailing by a score of 2–0. There were two men out and runners on second and third when Enrique Wilson came to bat. Wilson was mired in a terrible slump, entering the game zero for his last 26 at-bats. Additionally, he was hitting just .212 on the year with two outs and runners in scoring position. Meanwhile, the on-deck hitter, Einar Diaz, was a .421 stick with two outs and men in scoring position and .268 overall. Wilson had never received an intentional walk during his short big league career. Is now the time to give him a free pass?

Answer: It would seem an unlikely spot to use that strategy, but that's exactly what the Orioles' manager, Ray Miller, did. It failed when Diaz stroked a single to score both runners. The Indians cruised to a win.

Take a Pitch?

On June 23, 1999, Arizona was playing Cincinnati and found themselves trailing the Reds by a 9–5 score entering the final inning. The Diamondbacks began to claw their way back against Reds reliever Scott Williamson. By the time leadoff hitter Tony Womack came to the plate there was one man out and Bernard Gilkey, who had pinch-hit, was on base. More importantly, the score was narrowed to 9–7.

Now, Williamson doesn't walk many batters, but he had fallen behind to Gilkey. When the count ran to 3-and-0, Buck Showalter had a key decision to make. What did he do/What would you have done? Have Womack take a pitch—that is, stand in the box and refuse to swing at the next pitch?

Remember, with the number two and three hitters to follow, things were beginning to look promising. On the other hand, if you are convinced Williamson has to groove a pitch, to get a strike to avoid the walk, why take the bat out of Womack's hands? What's your call?

What happened: Womack actually took two pitches. He then battled Williamson for nine pitches in all before flying out harmlessly to left. When Jay Bell followed with a strikeout, the rally fell short. Still, most experts agree with what Arizona did.

Pitchout

Everyone knows a pitchout can be a smart call if you've either stolen the other team's signs or if you have a strong hunch the runner is going to be attempting a steal. Would you ever call for back-to-back pitchouts?

Answer: This strategy is quite rare, but it was done on August 14, 1999. Atlanta's manager, Bobby Cox, who once said of playing things by the book, "There is no book," was the man to make this call. With two men out, Adrian Beltre was on first base for the Los Angeles Dodgers. John Smoltz had an 0-and-2 count on the batter when Cox called for the first pitchout.

Nothing doing on the Dodgers' part, so Cox considered the situation. He had faith in Smoltz; after all, if they pitched out again and the runner didn't go, the count would go to 2-and-2, a situation Smoltz could handle, especially with two outs.

Plus, if the Dodgers were lulled into running, feeling the Braves simply wouldn't pitch out again, Atlanta could earn an easy out to end the inning. After all the philosophizing, the Braves did a second pitchout but the Dodgers, also considering many factors, did not send Beltre.

Deke 'Em?

Would you want your defensive players trying to decoy players from the other team, or is it just a waste of time (perhaps even a breech of baseball etiquette) at the major league level?

Answer: Nothing wrong with a good "deke." On August 7, 1999, two dupe plays were tried in a game; one didn't work.

Los Angeles had Raul Mondesi in right field versus the New York Mets. A batter singled sharply to right and, just about the time he reached first, Mondesi, who had already gloved the ball, pretended the ball got through his legs. He spun towards the outfield wall as if he was about to chase after the ball. Nice try, but the Mets were alert and the play failed.

Do You Throw behind a Runner?

A cardinal rule in baseball is: Don't throw behind a runner. If you do, and the runner is aggressive, the defense will pay the price for violating this rule. Ty Cobb would turn bases widely trying to lure a fielder to throw behind him—when the throw was made, Cobb was off and running, sliding safely into the next base. Is it ever advantageous to throw behind the runner?

Answer: Sure. There are always exceptions in baseball. In fact the second of the two August 7th decoys came on just such a play. A Kansas City Royal worked his deke to perfection against Brent Gates of the Minnesota Twins. Gates hit a routine single to right field where Jermaine Dye came up with it cleanly. Then, Dye glanced at second base as if that was where his throw would go.

Since Dye and his body language indicated a routine throw to his cutoff man, Gates felt secure in taking a wide turn around first. Should the ball be mishandled, Gates was ready to hustle to second. The only problem was, Gates was being conned; Dye threw behind him and although Gates scrambled back, it was too late—he was nabbed at first.

Manufacturing a Run

What's the best way to hustle into first base when attempting to beat out an infield hit? Should the runner go as fast as he can down the line and drive through the bag, or should he go hard then slide headfirst?

Answer: Most experts tell you never to slide. Omar Vizquel said, "I believe it's faster running through the bag, but Robbie [Alomar] doesn't think so. He's been using that [headfirst slide] play since he came into the big leagues."

Alomar, Vizquel's Cleveland teammate, verified that, "A lot of people have told me I shouldn't do it, but it's the way I play the game."

On June 5, 1999, Roberto Alomar not only used "his play," he dazzled the crowd with it. In the 11th inning of a game versus the Chicago Cubs, Alomar slashed a hard grounder to Mark Grace. The ball ate Grace up, hitting him in his chest. Alomar recalled, "It kind of took a bad hop." Grace then groped for the ball.

There, Alomar picks up the call, "He tried to throw it to the pitcher [Scott Sanders] who was covering first base. I dove and beat the throw. The pitcher missed the throw and the ball went maybe five feet away from him. I saw the ball was far enough where I could make it to second base. I went to second while the pitcher got the ball in four territory; he threw it way wide [of second] into left field. Henry Rodriquez caught the ball, but I was on third base already."

Now, a teammate said the key to the play was the fact that Alomar executed the rather unorthodox slide. Because of that, he was able to see the ball trickle away. So, as Alomar reported,

32

by the time the dust cleared, Alomar got what was tantamount to a triple on what could've been a routine groundout. All on hustle and instinct.

Alomar's analysis of the play was simple: "The pitcher didn't hustle. I think he was upset he didn't catch the ball. I took advantage." He added that he made his split-second decision to scamper because, "Hey, it's a tie game; let's make something happen."

It's no wonder a 1999 poll of American League managers conducted by a respected publication called *Baseball America* selected Alomar as the best base runner in his league; he frequently makes big plays and smart moves on the base paths. Indians manager Mike Hargrove said of Alomar, "He sees a lot of things that other players can't or won't see."

Your Move

Incidentally, with Alomar on third and only one out in that tie game, the Cubs manager had to make a desperate defensive move. What do you think it was? What would you have done?

Jim Riggleman intentionally walked the next two batters. He then directed his left fielder, Jose Hernandez, to play right behind second base, giving the Cubs a five-man infield. He knew a sacrifice fly would beat him, but a double play could end the inning—he had nothing to lose.

As it turned out, Wil Corero singled cleanly down the left field line to win it. Hargrove said the Cubs did the right thing: "If you hit a medium-to-deep flyball, the game is over anyway."

Run Wild? Depends upon the Runner

Now, if your were managing a team and the runner was John Olerud rather than Alomar, would you want him to be aggressive or conservative? In other words, test your big league knowledge, is Olerud a good, fast runner or not?

Answer: While he is a good runner in the sense that he is smart and won't run himself into a mistake, he is one of the slowest men at the big league level. So, you do like to see an Alomar, a Kenny Lofton, or a Roger Cedeno take calculated chances on the bases with their blazing speed and/or prowess, but not a runner like Olerud.

Olerud, Part II

Speaking of Olerud and Cedeno, consider this 1999 scenario. The Mets had Cedeno and Rickey Henderson on first and second with Olerud at the plate with one out. The count goes full to Olerud. Manager Bobby Valentine has to decide if he wants to put his runners in motion or not. Did he? Would you?

Answer: He did and you probably should, too, since that play makes sense on several levels. First of all, Olerud doesn't whiff too often, so a strike-him-out/throw-him-out double play doesn't seem likely. Secondly, the runners possess great speed,

so a double steal could result even if Olerud would strike out. Finally, if he does put the ball in play, having the runners on the go might eliminate an inning-ending double play.

Lay One Down

The *Baseball America* survey also picked the best bunters in each league. Now, if you were managing a 1999 team and could pick any three men based on their bunting ability, who would you go with? Clue: The poll's top three all came from the same team.

Answer: Based on managers' input, the best at laying down bunts were Cleveland's trio of: Omar Vizquel, followed by Kenny Lofton, then Roberto Alomar. All three can bunt for a sacrifice or for a hit.

How to Handle Juan Gonzalez—You Don't

On July 17th the Texas Rangers squared off against the Arizona Diamondbacks. Knowing Gonzalez is a strong pull hitter, what strategy might you deploy? Think about it, then read on to see what Arizona's manager Buck Showalter did.

What happened: The Diamondbacks skipper had his second baseman, Tony Womack, play to the left side of the second base bag. Facing a left side of the diamond stacked with three infielders, Gonzalez tattooed his 25th homer of the year, going over the shift. It was a case of making a smart move but getting negative results nevertheless.

The Great Garciaparra

On May 28 Boston's Nomar Garciaparra hit two home runs in the Red Sox game versus Cleveland. The next day Indians pitcher Bartolo Colon took a 1–0 lead into the eighth inning before trouble struck. First, Darren Lewis singled. Trot Nixon doubled, giving the Sox men at second and third. Jose Offerman then grounded out to second, scoring Lewis with the tying run.

At that point, manager Mike Hargrove had Colon issue an intentional walk to John Valentin. That set the stage for Cleveland's bullpen to become active. Southpaw Ricky Rincon was successful in retiring left-handed hitting Brian Daubach on a pop-up. Enter the next relief pitcher, Paul Shuey, a righty, to face the always-dangerous Garciaparra, who bats right handed. Clearly Hargrove was playing the percentages with his bullpen.

But, wait—in this situation will Cleveland walk Boston's All Star shortstop, or will Shuey and his blazing fastball go at him? Perhaps you'll have Shuey pitch to him, but offer nothing good to swing at; tempt him to chase a pitch out of the strike zone to end the inning?

Answer: This is yet another situation where caution seems to be in order. If you said walk or pitch around Garciaparra, you may have made the best decision. The Indians pitched to him and Shuey took him to a 2-and-2 count before Garciaparra ripped a hanging slider to give Boston a three-run homer and the lead they'd never relinquish.

Garciaparra One Day Later

The very next day Boston had two men out in the third inning of a scoreless game. Garciaparra again came to the plate and was on a torrid streak against Cleveland, with a total of three home runs in his last two games against them.

Runners were on second and third. So, with first base open, do you now give the .333 hitter (for 1999) a free pass, or is that poor baseball strategy?

What happened this time? The Indians did not walk him and the results were disastrous. Cleveland's starter that day, Dwight Gooden, saw his 2–1 pitch, a fastball, sail 437 feet. The game, in effect, was over; the final wound up being 4–2, Boston on top.

"I thought about walking him," said Hargrove, "but it's tough for me to intentionally walk someone in the third inning." Research indicates, however, that exactly one week earlier Hargrove had faced a man on second in the third inning with a two-out situation. In that very similar situation, he had ordered an intentional walk to Detroit's Frank Catalanotto.

Not only that, he had also given free passes to opponents in similar scenarios in the first inning of a game on April 25 and in the second inning of an April 11 contest.

Now, although Cleveland led the league in intentional walks served up (19) on the day of Garciaparra's fourth homer in three games against the Indians, Hargrove said "no" this time to such strategy and paid the price.

In his defense, and to show that managers are always thinking even if a decision goes awry, it should be noted that the batter after Garciaparra was also a tough out. As Hargrove put it, "They also had Troy O'Leary on deck and he's hit us well in the past." He was correct: O'Leary was hitting a cool .429 against the Indians in 1999 to Garciaparra's .364.

Again, right or wrong, managers have their reasons for moves. Furthermore, Hargrove is highly successful (don't forget his gut instinct call of the '95 A.L.C.S., sticking with Assenmacher—Chapter Two). Sometimes it's simply a case of "sometimes you win, sometimes..."

What's Up, Doc?

A final note regarding the Gooden–Garciaparra encounter: Rookie catcher Einar Diaz wanted Gooden to go with a breaking ball. Hargrove said Diaz wanted it "down and away, but Gooden wanted to throw a fastball. They talked about it and Doc threw the fastball to Garciaparra."

Ironically, Gooden had said earlier, "Going into the game he's the one guy you tell yourself you're not going to let beat you." Yet he also stated, "I never considered walking him." Some Cleveland fans said Hargrove should've taken charge and ordered exactly what he wanted done. Life as a manager is tough, as they're constantly second-guessed.

Interestingly, later in the season, in September, Gooden again faced Garciaparra in a situation that called for an intentional walk. This time the Indians did issue the free pass. Quickly, two things happened: first, the Cleveland crowd cheered the strategy (some sarcastically, others gratefully); second (and quite ironically), O'Leary stepped into the batter's box to face reliever Mark Langston and crushed the second pitch for a three-run homer. It was yet another case of "sometimes it seems like you just can't win."

Can You Take the Heat?

Even a manager's own player will often give him some flak. What would you do if you wore the manager's spikes on this one? Derek Bell wasn't hitting like his Astros expected. By July 18, his batting average was an anemic .245. Not long after that his strikeout total reached an alarming 100. Would you continue to hit him second, or would you feel that by that stage of the season it was time to make a move?

Answer: His manager, Larry Dierker, dropped Bell from his usual two-spot in the batting order all the way down to the sixth hole. Bell fumed, "It isn't right, I've been battling all year and getting key hits for the team and doing other things in the second slot. It's like a slap in the face, dropping me all the way down...I strike out a lot, but I do a lot of things to help this team win. I'm not a crybaby, but damn."

Now, to most fans a crybaby is exactly what he was. Why not try harder instead of complaining? Dierker said, "I try not to be authoritarian, but somebody has to make out the lineup card. I'm just doing what I think is best for the team."

Did you, like Dierker, have the guts to make the switch? Later, Bell batted in other slots, including clean-up, but wound up with a disappointing season (.236, 12 HR, 66 RBI, 129 strikeouts).

To Run or Not to Run

Then there was the managerial move that brought some grief to the highly respected Tony LaRussa of the St. Louis Cardinals. On the 14th of June, he had 40-year-old Willie McGee try to steal with one out in the bottom of the tenth inning. The Cardinals trailed 3–1 at the time, and McGee was gunned down. Can you think of a reason why the move made sense and reason(s) why it seemed to be bad strategy?

Answers: LaRussa reasoned having McGee in motion would keep his team out of a double play. On the debit side, when McGee was retired, the batter at the plate no longer represented the tying run. Worse, perhaps, the game ended with Mark McGwire on deck; he was robbed of a chance to swing in a key situation.

To Run or Not to Run, Part II

Imagine you are manager Bobby Cox, a huge driving force behind the 1990s success of the Atlanta Braves and, in fact, the winningest manager of that decade (with 900 victories). Now, you're playing Arizona and it's the seventh inning. You lead in this one, 7–3, and have catcher Javy Lopez on first. Lopez is not a throwback to what fans often think of when they think of catchers. That is to say, Lopez is very athletic and, at 6' 3", 200 pounds, quite trim (unlike the stereotypical stout and slow catchers of days gone by). Lopez even stole five bases in 1998. The Diamondbacks wouldn't be expecting a steal in this situation, so, do you let him run?

Answer: It seems unwise to send him, especially in retrospect. Using hindsight, it's clear to see his attempted steal back on June 20, 1999, was ill-fated. Lopez slid hard into second base and injured himself badly enough that he had to be placed on the disabled list. Lopez defended his romp by saying baseball should be played hard at all times.

Part 2

YOU'RE THE FRONT OFFICE —THE GENERAL MANAGER

Fans not only love to play the armchair manager game, they also love to argue trades and discuss which ball players are the best at their position. Here you have a chance to become, in effect, the general manager of an imaginary club and to build a team. So, go to it!

Chapter Four

BUILDING YOUR TEAM

Imagine you're putting together a solid club. Experts say a great defensive team must be rock solid up the middle. With that in mind, respond to the following questions and build a team that can handle the leather with skill.

Behind the Plate

If you could start a team from scratch and have any player in baseball behind the plate, which man would you choose? Here are a few names to help you decide:

Charles Johnson   Ivan Rodriguez   Brad Ausmus
Javy Lopeze   Mike Piazza

Answer: Ask any expert today and you'll get the same reply —Ivan Rodriguez is the best catcher since Johnny Bench. In fact, some even contend that he's better than the Hall-of-

Famer. *USA Today* did a survey naming the greatest defensive players, position by position, of the last 25 years. They went with Rodriguez over Bench. Maybe they're right. After all, in 1998, Rodriguez gunned out a season record 52.5 percent of the runners who tried to steal on him (this statistic has been kept now since 1989; not back to the days of Bench). Nevertheless, a success rate of 50 percent or better is simply unheard of! Not for this standout, though—in 1999 he improved upon his record and threw out 54.2% of those too bold or foolish to know you shouldn't try to steal against Rodriguez. As of the end of 1999, he had, as a matter of fact, thrown out 50% or better for three straight years. Further, from 1995–1999, his average for throwing out would-be base-burglars was exactly 50%—for a five-year span! Not only that, 1999 marked the fifth straight year that his caught-stealing rate ranked number one in the entire majors.

Throwing out around 33–35% of enemy runners is pretty good, upwards around 40% is staggering, but, again, 50% is simply unthinkable. For his entire career through 1999 Rodrigues's rate of gunning down the enemy was an astronomical 46.9%. Plus, he had only one passed ball in 1999 (#1 in the majors) to go with his 10 pickoffs. You would think opposing runners would know better than to mess with "Pudge". After all, from 1996 to 1999, he averaged almost 10 pickoffs each season. He is, as you might expect, a perennial Gold Glove winner (with eight straight trophies through 1999). His prowess prompted Detroit Manager Larry Parrish to say, "His bad throws are other guys' good throws."

Rodriguez himself downplays all of that. "I'm just another player in the game and I gotta come here every day to do my job." When asked what other catchers he respects, "Pudge" replied, "I respect every catcher because we are all big leaguers, we're all good players."

Final note: all the men on the list (with the exception of Piazza) are considered to be fine defensive catchers, but, again, Rodriguez is pretty much in a class all his own. If you went with Johnson, don't feel bad. Many experts say that Johnson can give Rodriguez a bit of a run for his money.

Shortstop Selection

This time the rules are changed a bit. You must pick a young shortstop for your squad. By young, we'll go with an age of 25 or below, which leaves out such scintillating shortstops as Rey Ordonez. This man entered the 2000 season with a major league record string of 100 errorless games played at short. If you listened to veteran reliever Jesse Orosco, you would definitely want to select Ordonez, who won his third straight Gold Glove in 1999 based on just four errors, none after June 13th. During a 1998 interview, when Orosco played for the Orioles, he was asked what was the most amazing thing he'd ever seen on a diamond. He replied, "Every time I see Rey Ordonez make a play, it's an unbelievable play. That kid's impressive and when I played against him in New York when we went down there, I told him personally, 'It's just a pleasure watching you.' And it really is; it's amazing." While you can't go with Ordonez, you can, however, go with one of these four:

Deivi Cruz	Mike Caruso
Miguel Tejada	Neifi Perez

The Pick

Of course if you could pick from any shortstop at all, the wisest choices would include men such as Derek Jeter, Nomar Garciaparra, and Alex Rodriguez, as they blend both offense and defense into their game (not to mention Omar Vizquel, yet another standout). Jeter committed just nine errors in 1998 and 14 the following year, probably making him the best of the trio when emphasizing defense. Garciaparra had 17 errors in 1999 to Rodriguez's 14. Amazingly, three of the four star shortstops mentioned are still relatively young yet have experience as well. Only Vizquel is over 27, at 33 years of age.

While it's very difficult to project a young player's future, of the men listed in the multiple choice, we'll go with the 24-year-old Perez. He's got such good, soft hands, plus fine range, and a strong arm, you've just got to like him. In 1998 he took part in 128 double plays, which placed him in a tie for the eighth most D.P.'s ever turned by a shortstop in a single season. He did have 20 errors in 1998, but then that figure dropped down to 14 the next season, when he also took part in 124 D.P.'s. Plus, he may even get steadier in the future —perhaps more so than the others on the list. He may not make the spectacular play as well as some of the others above, but he'll do.

If you want the kind of player who will make the dramatic play, you might go with Tejada and his great range—one expert said it's the best in the American League, but Tejada did have 26 errors in '98, with 21 in '99. Some scouts still like Caruso, who is capable of making scintillating plays yet will boot some routine ones (he had 35 E's in '98, then 24 in '99, which upset the White Sox). A plus for Caruso is his age, 22. He is also very quick, and that's a skill that really can't be taught. Others like Cruz and his low error total in 1999 (12).

Keep in mind, young players' error totals can be misleading. Many players who went on to become all-time greats often had fielding troubles early on. Consider, for example, other shortstops such as Alan Trammell, who had 26 errors when he was 21. Then there was Robin Yount. During the season he turned 20, some observers thought he was a butcher; he was guilty of committing 44 errors. Toss in Derek Jeter, who, as good as he is now, made a mind-reeling 56 errors one year in the minors! Trammell said, "You're gonna boot some balls, that's the way it is. But if you eliminate the careless errors, you'll be okay." He stressed careless ones are often the poor, casual throws that, for example, pull the first baseman off the bag. Improvement in areas such as those bad throws comes with age. "You get more comfortable as years go on," said the Tigers great. "Infielders get around 15 errors a year—that's pretty good. When you get up to 25 errors, a lot could have not occurred." Keep all that in mind as you select your shortstop of the future.

Finish Your Infield

Moving now to second base, you have this choice: you may select any National League player. If you were allowed to pick a American Leaguer, it's a no-brainer—Robby Alomar is the best. In 1999 he won his eighth Gold Glove; that tied him with Frank White and Bill Mazeroski for the second most by a second baseman. It also left him just one Gold Glove shy of tying the all-time record held by Ryne Sandberg. Clearly, he's in great company.

Orosco commented that, like his experience with Ordonez, playing with Alomar in Baltimore was great "after playing against Robby Alomar all those years and then I come here [to Baltimore in 1998] and say to myself, 'Wow! All those plays he's made and now I get to see it everyday'—it's pretty amazing." If you want help in selecting a National League star, you might consider these choices:

Mickey Morandini	Bret Boone	Pokey Reese
Craig Biggio	Edgardo Alfonzo	

Answer: We just have to hedge a bit since all five are fine choices. If you want to go with a long track record, Biggio may be your best bet. Even Boone admits Biggio is the best all-around second baseman in baseball. While Boone also admires Alfonzo and Jay Bell, he says Biggio is the man. Although Biggio, a former catcher, is 34, he won four consecutive Gold Glove awards from 1994 through 1997. The 1999 bench coach of the Chicago White Sox, Joe Nossek said, "One of my favorite players is Biggio, not only offensively, but defensively he gives you everything he's got, nine innings, every time he goes out there." Fellow White Sox coach Von Joshua agreed, "No question about it, Biggio. Boone is not consistent enough for me. He's a good second baseman, but Biggio's the best."

Boone has his supporters, though. He has a great first step, helping him range far with his glove. Those skills go well with his fine hands. Put all that together, and it's no wonder he won his first Gold Glove in 1998. Not only that, 1997 was, in some ways, even better. That was the year he established the big league record for the best fielding percentage in a season by a second baseman, a sterling .997 mark. In fact, he entered the 1999 season with the third-best fielding percentage at second base of all time (although he didn't have enough games played at that time to be listed in the record books).

If you want to build more for the future, Reese looks real good. He's four years younger than Boone, who is 30 years old. Reese was positively brilliant in 1999 with an errorless streak of 67 games and 314 chances. Not only that, he had just one error all year up to July 18th and wound up with just seven. It's little wonder, then, that he copped his first Gold Glove in 1999. In 1999, Phil Garner, who played second base for most of his big league career, said, "Right now, the guy who's burst on the scene this year that you have to give a lot of credit to is Pokey Reese. What's made him stand out, besides being a solid glove man, is his range. It's better than most guys'." When asked if that could be because Reese is a converted shortstop, Garner replied, "It's because he's got great speed. He's got a jet in his heinie, that's what it is. I think he could still play shortstop, but he's not going to play ahead of Barry Larkin [at Cincinnati]."

Von Joshua added, "Reese can play. You got a guy who's a shortstop moving over to second. If he had that range at shortstop, just think what kind of range he's going to have at second. Outstanding." You should also give strong consideration to Alfonzo, who switched to second base in 1999 from what had been his normal position, third base, where he was ranked among the best. In his first full year at second he committed only five errors. He's one of the main reasons the 1999 Mets set a new big league record by committing an all-time low 33 errors by their infield (a remarkable 12 less than the previous record holder, the 1964 Orioles). On October 13th of 1999, during the N.L.C.S., he committed his first fielding error on a grounder all year long. He's quick, has soft hands and a strong arm—a total defensive package. Many felt he deserved the 1999 Gold Glove award. Ordonez stated, "It was an injustice. Edgardo had an awesome year defensively." If he had won it, the Mets would have tied a record (set by the 1971 Orioles and the Orioles of 1973–75) by having three Gold Glove winners in their infield.

Morandini said that if he had to go with a young second sacker, he'd also have to take a look at "Ron Belliard up in Milwaukee. I think he's going to be a good one, and obviously, Pokey Reese. He's made the transition from shortstop real nice. Then there's the kid from Kansas City, Carlos Febles, he looks like he's a real good defensive player, too. Luis Castillo with the Marlins, he's a young player, too. There are a lot of young second basemen coming up, making an impact."

If forced to make a pick, go with Biggio for now and Reese or Alfonzo for the immediate future.

The Best D.P. Duo

Now, if you could take any double-play combination active in 1999, regardless of age, what would your decision be? Clue: Almost any expert approached agrees on this American League duo. They played as teammates for the first time in 1999.

Answer: The dream D.P. duet is Cleveland's Omar Vizquel and Roberto Alomar. Some baseball observers have gone so far as to say they are, based upon pure skills, the best double-play duo ever. In 1999, their first year as a combo, their dazzling defensive gems could fill up two or three episodes of "This Week in Baseball." In that spectacular season Alomar took part in 102 double plays while posting a sparkling .992 fielding percentage, tops in his league. Alomar's range and quickness are unmatched. Entering the 2000 season, Alomar's .987 fielding percentage ranked number one for all the second basemen who ever played in the American League. Over his lifetime he had accepted 5,964 total chances while being guilty of only 76 errors—a total some second basemen could reach in, say, three or four seasons. In 1999 his fielding percentage was a superlative .992, but that's not all. In 1992 he made only five errors to tie the all-time American League single-season record for second basemen. He also once played in 104 consecutive errorless games, also an American League record for players at that demanding position.

As for the smooth Vizquel, he's so confident of his ability, he'll even catch hard-hit balls in his bare hand then throw out a befuddled runner. And when it comes to making the routine plays, like Alomar he makes it look oh, so easy. Unafraid to take chances, Vizquel is still able to preserve his lofty lifetime fielding percentage. It stood at .981 going into 2000, the best ever for any shortstop in the history of the game when based on having played 1,000 or more contests. In fact, in 1998 he posted a fielding percentage of .993 with only 5 errors over his 720 total chances accepted. That ranks #2 for a single season throughout the history of the game. Further, only three shortstops have ever won more Gold Gloves than Vizquel: legendary Ozzie Smith (with 13 won consecutively), Luis Aparicio (9), and Mark Belanger (8). In 1999, Vizquel set an American League record when he won his seventh Gold Glove in a row. Clearly, Indians pitchers loved having Alomar and Vizquel behind them, and fans loved seeing their acrobatic plays.

Chapter Five

Defenders in the Outfield

You've made a good start, but every position is important in putting together a winning team. You still have more decisions to make, so let's look to the outfield.

Center Field

For this spot, conceding the obvious pick of Ken Griffey, Jr., a 10-time Gold Glove winner (all in a row) through 1999, there is only one other man you, as a manager, should consider. Here are some clues: The smooth outfielder is under 25. He's a National Leaguer who covers a whole lot of ground. In 1998, his real-life manager Bobby Cox said this man was one of the best center fielders he'd ever seen. He was born in Curacao and made a very impressive World Series debut, hitting home runs in his first two Series at-bats, an unprecedented feat. Who is he?

Answer: Atlanta's Andruw Jones, a man still so young, 22, it's hard to imagine he got so good so fast. He has all the defensive skills you could ask for, including a rifle arm. Some say his arm is better than Griffey's from center field. Thus, he probably has the best arm of any center fielder in the game. In 1996 this manchild pole-vaulted from Class A baseball to the majors in just a staggering two short months. Then, two years later, he won a Gold Glove based on committing a mere two errors while racking up 413 putouts. In 1999 he added more hardware to his trophy case, winning another Gold Glove. In addition, he plays a very shallow center. They say the great ones play in, rather than play deep, because such men have supreme confidence that they can go back for a ball, a prowess much more difficult than playing deep and coming in for balls. Tris Speaker, for example, loved to play so shallow, he was not too far behind second base. That didn't stop him from recording 450 lifetime assists, the best ever, plus an all-time American League high of 35 in one season. He also had more American League putouts (6,794) than anyone else. Perhaps most interesting, though, is the fact that he chalked up 135 double plays from center field (the all-time record), including another record six unassisted double plays for his career. Therefore, it wasn't uncommon for Speaker to come in on, say, a sinking line drive, snag it, then dash to second base to retire the runner who had been on second but had made the mistake of thinking the ball just couldn't be caught. Once that runner took off, trying to score on what he thought would be a single, he was doomed. Speaker had the speed and savvy to complete the twin killing. On other occasions, Speaker would sneak in behind a runner who was leading off second. The pitcher would swivel then nail the daring runner in a most unusual pickoff.

'USA Today' Survey

In April of 1999, when *USA Today* ran the article featuring the greatest defensive players of the last 25 years, their panel of 12 experts listed many of the men from our choices earlier.

As mentioned, not only was Ivan Rodriguez their selection as the best catcher since 1974, they even went with him over the immortal Johnny Bench. Going up the middle on defense, they picked Vizquel among the top four shortstops and Roberto Alomar as the best at second. Ken Griffey, Jr., was tops in center field, naturally. Andruw Jones, with only two years' experience at that time, was among the four greatest center fielders.

Now, if you had to go with a good fielding pitcher to finish off your fledgling team's up-the-middle defense, who would you name?

Answer: Our pick, who was also the *USA Today* selection, is Greg Maddux. Mike Mussina is a tempting thought with his four Gold Gloves, but Maddux owned nine straight Gold

Gloves as of the 1999 survey. Then, when he won the award again in 1999, he completed a monopoly on the trophy, having won it each year in the decade of the 1990s. In fact, that broke a tie he had had with Bob Gibson for the most Gold Gloves ever by a National League pitcher (Jim Kaat has the overall record with 16).

The Rest of the Defense

While left and right field may not be as important as center, think of the two other players that you'd like to have to round out your strong defensive outfield. Here are a few clues concerning our picks: Legendary manager Sparky Anderson called the left fielder in question "the best I've ever seen out there." He shook his head in wonderment as he spoke those words; and, remember, Anderson has seen a lot of left fielders come and go. The *USA Today* survey listed this man as being better than Dave Winfield and even Carl Yastrzemski in left. Not only does he excel on defense, he is a bona fide slugger who can also hit for average as well as steal a ton of bases. Final clues—He was born in 1964 and he hits and throws lefty. Meanwhile, the active right fielder is only 24 years old. A native of the Dominican Republic (no, it's not Sammy Sosa—he's 31), thanks to a trade this man got to play on the same team with his brother (who came from the Los Angeles Dodgers) for the first time at the major league level in 1998. Who is he?

Answers: The left fielder, and nobody seems to argue this point, is Barry Bonds. Through 1998 he won an impressive eight Gold Gloves. Further testimony to Bond's ability comes from Tony Gwynn, who once said that the majority of his hits go to left field. If defenses know that, why don't they cheat in on him in left to deny him the countless stinging line drives and well-placed bloopers he dumps into his opposite field? Gwynn, who hit higher than any man in the 1990s at .344, said, "It's funny, every team is different. Some try to take hits up the middle away from you, or take away something else.

Barry Bonds tries to take it away from me [in left], but it takes guts and talent to do that. Bonds is the only left fielder in the National League who has the guts to come in and say, 'I dare you to hit it over my head.' In my career I only did it once." So, like Speaker, Bonds is not afraid to play shallow.

Chicago great Billy Williams roamed left field for nearly twenty years, so his opinion counts highly. "I was out in Oakland when Rickey Henderson played left field. I've seen guys get to the line quick, but there was nobody quicker than Rickey Henderson, taking away doubles—he was good at that.

"But when you look at Barry playing the outfield, he's worked hard. He doesn't have a strong arm, but he charges the ball and he makes great plays in the outfield. I think with his experience now, knowing where hitters hit the ball, he gets himself in good position to make the plays. He's just become a great left fielder," Williams summed up.

The right field situation is a bit more cloudy, but we'll go with Vladimir Guerrero or Larry Walker over other fine possibilities. Those men would include players such as Brian Jordan, who has one of the top five arms in the game now. B.J. Surhoff added, "Sean Green is a very good right fielder. He's not only up-and-coming, he's here and [continuing] on the way up." Surhoff was right; Green captured his first Gold Glove award in 1999.

Don't forget Raul Mondesi, either. On his right biceps he has a tattoo depicting a cannon, perfectly symbolizing his throwing prowess. In 1994 and 1995, he threw out 16 runners to twice lead the league. He captured Gold Gloves in 1995 and 1997. Jesse Orosco likes O'Neill and Buhner for American League right fielders, saying, "O'Neill is steady; Buhner probably has an edge for the arm."

If you were considering how strong a man's arm is, Manny Ramirez deserves some consideration, although he is erratic and seemingly absentminded at times. Still, Cleveland coach Jeff Newman said Ramirez is his pick as the best in the league. "People talk [negatively] about him, but I tell you what, he makes all the plays, he always hits his cutoff man, he makes

53

good, strong throws, and I bet he's in the top bracket of assists this year. Manny has made some mistakes out there but, all in all, he plays a very good right field." Newman was wrong, though, concerning assists, as Ramirez had seven in 1999, a far cry from the outfield leaders' total of 17 registered by Jermaine Dye and Albert Belle. Meanwhile, Guerrero is the kind of guy everybody raves about. Some even say he has the best arm in all of baseball. The peculiar thing about Guerrero is his error totals have been high thus far for the early stage of his career, but experts tout his defensive play regardless. In his first full season, 1997, he committed 12 errors (versus 10 assists). The next two years his totals were 17 errors (with nine assists) and 19 errors (15 assists). By mid-August of 1999, he had been on pace to commit 20 errors—no outfielder had done that dubious feat since way back in 1935. When the season ended, his 19 miscues tied for the most by an outfielder in the post-World War II era (only Lou Brock in 1966 and Chili Davis in 1988 made as many errors).

Listen, though, to the praise. Alex Ochoa, who possesses a fine outfield arm himself, said, "He has a great arm, he can throw from anywhere and any position. It's one of those things guys are born with and you gotta respect them when they get the ball."

Longtime coach Sam Perlozzo said, "There's a lot more to it than a strong arm. I've seen some guys with average arms who charge the ball really well and are really accurate who are better." One such example might be Paul O'Neill: "He's just an all-round good outfielder; he doesn't make many mistakes, he's very accurate, he never misses a cutoff man, and he has a pretty good arm. Guerrero does have a cannon, but he can be erratic." Still, the nod here goes to Guerrero and Larry Walker in a photo-finish call.

Walker deserves respect for his many skills. He gets that respect from fans and from his peers. In 1999 managers and coaches voted to give Walker his fifth Gold Glove. Even though he played in only 114 contests in right field, he still wound up tied for sixth in his league with 13 outfield assists— and that includes seven runners he fired out at the plate!

Back to the Corners

Texas Rangers standout Rafael Palmeiro was the pick of Jeff Newman as the best at first in the American League. Former teammate in Baltimore Mike Bordick concurred, "He's real good at first; he's won some Gold Gloves over there. I think his defensive ability gets overlooked because of his bat." Interestingly, towards the end of the 1999 season Palmeiro was asked who the best was at first. Since he had been the D.H. for most of that season, he was given the chance to watch his backup, Lee Stevens, play first. Palmeiro felt Stevens deserved the Gold Glove, saying Stevens "has played really, really well." A Texas coach, Bucky Dent, agreed completely, saying, "I haven't seen anyone pick the ball out of the dirt better than this guy. There is nobody better." Ironically, though, about two months later Palmeiro won his third straight Gold Glove (one error in 275 chances) despite playing first only 28 games. Meanwhile, Jesse Orosco gave his opinion: "David Segui is the best glove. Brogna's the best in the National League." Still, don't forget Rico Brogna, who is also coming on strong. Then there's Sean Casey. In 1999, then 24 years old, he went 67 straight games without an error. Billy Williams said he felt Grace and Snow are "two of the guys that are really outstanding with the glove. The measure of a good first baseman is when he makes that 3–6–3 double play. You have to be quick, you have to concentrate on picking the ball up and making a good throw to second base, then you got to get back to the bag. You have to have good agility over there."

Among active players, only Mark Grace made the *USA Today* survey for great glove work. Still, J.T. Snow is great around the bag and owns five Gold Gloves (all in a row) through 1999. Like Williams, Von Joshua couldn't decide, but praised two men: "J.T. Snow reminds me a lot of Wes Parker. Very soft hands. Snow's better than Parker with his range. Grace gets the nod over Snow probably." He paused, then amended that judgment to "It's a toss-up. They're in a class by themselves."

Bill Pulsipher, a pitcher with the Milwaukee Brewers in 1999, said there are so many great fielders, but Jeff Bagwell and Grace came quickly to mind. Sean Berry says he likes Grace (who doesn't?) and how he plays the position, and agrees Snow is great. All things considered, our pick is Snow.

But what about third base? Who would your player be at the hot corner? Remember, the player must be active.

Answer: Until around 1998 or 1999, an automatic pick might well have been Ken Caminiti. However, as Von Joshua noted, due to age and injuries, he has slipped a bit. Still, he does own three Gold Gloves and he has a cannon for an arm.

All things considered, though, veteran pitcher Pulsipher rattled off many legitimate picks. He said, "It's tough because there are a lot of really good players at third. Obviously Jeff Cirillo is a great defensive ballplayer. Matt Williams is a great defensive player, Robin Ventura; I mean it's tough." Cirillo, for instance, took part in 45 double plays in 1998 to tie the all-time National League season record. Meanwhile, Pulsipher acknowledged Scott Rolen is looking good as well. Other experts mentioned names such as Scott Brosius and Vinny Castilla. If forced to pick one man, we simply can't. So, we'll go with Williams and his fine track record to go along with Ventura, who won his sixth Gold Glove in 1999, giving his Mets Gold Glovers at both spots on the left side of the infield.

Another point Pulsipher made is, "I don't think that there is a 'best', I think everybody does things differently. If you play with a guy, you're more likely to say that he's the best, because you get to see him every day. Just like when I played with Rey Ordonez—I can't see anybody being better than him at shortstop."

Mike Bordick said, "When you think of guys who just seem natural and fluid at a reaction position, Matt Williams is one who sticks out." Meanwhile, in 1999 Jeff Newman said, "Travis Fryman, when he's healthy, is fantastic."

In 1998, Fryman replaced Williams at third for the Indians. By 1999 he was named, in a survey taken of big league managers, as the top glove man at third in the American League. Nobody said these decisions would be easy.

Part 3
YOU'RE THE BASEBALL COMMISSIONER OR LEAGUE PRESIDENT

In this section of the book we'll imagine you have the power to render decisions on vital baseball matters that typically make their way to the top of baseball's hierarchy. In other words, you are, in some cases, the National or American League President, or, in other cases, the Commissioner of Baseball. Are you up to the task?

Chapter Six

REAL CASES FROM THE PAST

Many fans who follow the game imagine scenarios with them as decision-maker. For example, upon hearing that, say, Albert Belle was suspended for three days for yet another controversy, many people find themselves muttering, "If it was up to me, I'd have dealt with him more severely."

The Scenario

Not only do fans engage in such thinking—at least one former commissioner does, too. Bowie Kuhn, who served as baseball's leader from 1969 to 1984, stated he still skims the sports pages, reads about the latest controversies, and then, "Every morning I make my decision what I think should be done after reading the story." He then added, "There's just no one listening to me anymore."

In 1998, then San Francisco pitcher Orel Hershiser got caught up in such a situation. When the Florida Marlins engineered a swap with the Los Angeles Dodgers for their superstar catcher Mike Piazza, only to ship him to the Mets shortly thereafter, Hershiser felt the trades weren't ones Florida was making with good intentions (more on this in an upcoming problem for your consideration).

At the time, Gene "Bud" Selig was sitting atop baseball's power pyramid, although he didn't officially occupy the office of the commissioner.

Hershiser commented on the Floridian trades and on Selig's approval of the deal. The veteran pitcher believed the trade would have been nullified "if we had a real, genuine commissioner."

Although the trade did stand, Hershiser was correct in stating a commissioner does have the power to veto a major league player transaction. With that in mind, move on to the next scenario and accept your first challenge as baseball's head honcho.

Two Transaction That Were Voided

Charlie O. Finley was the owner of the Oakland A's during their glory years of the 1970s. His players won the World Series three consecutive seasons from 1972 to 1974, a feat no team has since duplicated.

By the time the 1976 season rolled around, Finley decided it was time to make some moves. First of all, he realized several of his players could soon leave the A's as they were about to become free agents. Since these men were in their prime, why not do some profit-taking, he figured. Finley, therefore, decided to dump the salaries of three of his stars. On top of that, by selling the three players instead of trading them, he'd make even more cash.

So, Finley was all set to ship starting pitcher Vida Blue to the New York Yankees and outfielder Joe Rudi along with reliever Rollie Fingers to the Boston Red Sox. In return he'd collect a cool $3.5 million, then a great deal of loot (a million each for Fingers and Rudi, a million and a half for Blue).

But wait. Along came Commissioner Bowie Kuhn to stop the deals, saying they would be detrimental to the game of baseball. For years, when a commissioner wanted to make a ruling in which there seemed to be no precedent, he would invoke an old phrase: "I'm acting in the best interest of baseball." Kuhn was no exception; those words tumbled out of his mouth in making this ruling. In fact, he added that the sales were "devastating to baseball's reputation for integrity and to public confidence in the game." Think about it. How would you have ruled?

Incidentally, if you agreed with Kuhn, you probably made the wise choice. After losing Round #1 to Kuhn, Finley took

59

him to court, insisting an owner should have the right to sell his players. The court ruled Kuhn's decision would stand. A few years later Finley sold his team, getting out of the game entirely.

Back to Florida

Getting back to the Florida situation involving the Piazza blockbuster swap: was Hershiser correct about the need for intervention by a "real, genuine" commissioner? Before you can rule, you'll need much more information.

The whole situation began not long after the Marlins won the 1997 World Series. On November 18 of that year, they unloaded outfielder Devon White and their superb closer out of the bullpen, Robb Nen, in two separate deals. Two days later they jettisoned more salary by sending Jeff Conine on his way.

That was bad enough for Marlins boosters, but some very nasty stuff began to hit the fan in mid-December when they traded their ace pitcher, Kevin Brown, to the San Diego Padres. Brown would go 18–7 with a minuscule 2.37 E.R.A. for San Diego, leading them to the World Series. Between November 20 and early February of the next year, Florida also got rid of Ed Vosberg, Al Leiter, Dennis Cook, and Kurt Abbott. In each instance the Marlins picked up little-known, inexpensive players.

When spring rolled around, the Marlins began to make more moves. On May 15, 1998, they dealt five players, including such luminaries as Gary Sheffield, Bobby Bonilla, and Gold Glove catcher Charles Johnson, for Mike Piazza and Todd Zeile.

Exactly a week later they threw Piazza and his huge salary overboard like so much ballast. They sent him packing to the New York Mets for a young, promising player named Preston Wilson and a minor leaguer.

Like many fans and experts, Hershiser believed that the owner of the Marlins, Wayne Huizengas, having won the

World Series just a scant year earlier, was cleaning house in a cost-cutting coup.

Huizengas contended his franchise was losing money and that he simply had to make the multitude of player moves.

Now, while it's clear the trades were consummated, would you have intervened? In case you're curious, here are some final points on the Florida debacle.

Kuhn said that if he were still commissioner he would have done the following: 1) Once it became apparent the Marlins were sweeping players out the door (in November of 1997), he would have forced them to get approval of any transaction. 2) As for the huge trade with the Dodgers, he would have delayed the trade considering the logic behind the move. He would also have considered denying the trade altogether.

Kuhn said he would have wanted to know for sure that the team was losing as much money as they claimed, and that they were truly attempting to build for the future. Kuhn said, "Someone would have to satisfy me that this was a long-term look at building the team. The rapidity with which they first built a rather expensive ball club and then carried out its dismantling is troublesome."

Kuhn also pointed out a key difference between what Florida was doing and what Finley tried to do with Blue, Rudi, and Fingers: the Marlins were making trades; Finley was selling players like a butcher peddles prime rib.

"When I dealt with Finley," said Kuhn, "he was liquidating his franchise. Finley was saying, 'I can't play with the big boys, I'm getting out.' On a much larger scale, the Marlins are looking at a similar situation.

"They're saying, 'Well, we can build a great team,' just as Finley did. But unfortunately, the economics didn't work in South Florida. The question is why they didn't. I don't know the answer, but if I were commissioner, I sure would." Like Hershiser, Kuhn felt the need for a full-fledged commissioner.

If that commissioner were you, and if you said you would have negated the Florida trades, or at least looked into them more closely, hats off to you.

Finley versus Kuhn, Part II

Here's another chance for you to rule on the best interest of baseball. It's October 14, time for the second game of the 1973 World Series between the Oakland A's and the New York Mets. Mike Andrews, a backup second baseman for the A's, entered the game in the eighth inning. Later, in the twelfth, the Mets won the game due to Andrews's presence in the game. New York had a one-run lead, the bases loaded, and two men out. The next batter, John Milner, hit a routine ground ball to Andrews. The ball scooted under his glove and between his legs, allowing two runs to cross the plate. Jerry Grote followed with another grounder to Andrews, who made a bad throw to first for yet another error and another Mets run. Those three insurance runs proved to be the difference in this frantic 10–7, four-hour-and-13-minute contest.

Finley was so upset with Andrews, he wanted to cut him from the squad immediately. Realizing this couldn't be done, Finley placed the healthy Andrews on the disabled list and sent him home. If you were Commissioner Kuhn, what would you do concerning this situation?

What happened: Realizing the move made by Finley was a sham, Kuhn ruled that Andrews be reinstated for the next game. Although Oakland manager Dick Williams didn't use Andrews in that contest, he did send him up to pinch-hit in the fourth game of the Series. When Andrews appeared out of the dugout to pinch-hit in the eighth inning, he received a rousing standing ovation.

Infamous Brawl

One of the most outrageous brawls in sports history took place on August 22, 1965, between bitter baseball rivals the Dodgers and the Giants. It all started when Juan Marichal of the Giants was in the batter's box. Opposing pitcher Sandy Koufax delivered a pitch to catcher Johnny Roseboro. At that point Roseboro threw the ball back to Koufax, but Marichal claimed the throw was close to his head and had been zipped there intentionally. In fact, he said, the ball grazed his ear. That was enough to trigger a wild one. Marichal attacked Roseboro using his bat. One blow opened up a nasty cut on Roseboro's head. How does this compare to other baseball infractions such as loading up a baseball? What's your ruling on Marichal's egregious brutality?

Now, compare your decision to what happened. Marichal was given a monetary fine as well as a suspension. He was banned from baseball for a nine-game period of time. The fine was in the amount of $1,750. Of course, players in that era didn't receive anywhere near the kind of money players now get, so we won't argue too much about the fine. However, many people feel Marichal should've been given a longer suspension.

Many people also believe Marichal's actions that day caused voters for the Hall of Fame to deny him entry into Cooperstown for several years. He was eligible for voting in 1980, and his statistics justified going in on the first ballot, but he didn't get inducted until 1983.

Brawl #2

On August 12, 1984, the San Diego Padres were playing at Atlanta. The very first pitch of the game from colorful Braves pitcher Pascual Perez bore in on Alan Wiggins, getting him in his back. That set a very ugly stage and it was time to cry havoc. Before the night was through, San Diego retaliated by throwing at Perez in each of his four at-bats.

After a while, Perez was virtually jumping out of the box before the pitch was delivered. Two clear-the-bench brawls ensued. Several fans even joined in on the melee, always a dangerous situation. By the end of the night, 19 players were ejected from the contest. Perhaps the biggest culprit, in the eyes of the National League president, was Padres manager Dick Williams, who orchestrated the vendetta on Perez. What punishment do you feel he deserved?

Answer: Williams was dealt with harshly. He received a $10,000 fine (pretty stiff even now) and was suspended for 10 days as well.

Manager for a Day

Ted Turner, who some feel has an ego as big as his financial empire, once thought he could actually manage a big league team. Perhaps he was thinking, "How tough can it be?" At any rate, on May 11, 1977, with his team, the Atlanta Braves, bogged down in last place with a pathetic 8–21 win-loss record, Turner told manager Dave Bristol he wanted him to leave the team temporarily. The Braves owner said Bristol was to take a ten-day scouting trip. Turner, in the meantime, would run the team.

Adorned in the stylish threads of the Braves, Turner sat in the dugout for a game versus the Pittsburgh Pirates. At the conclusion of the game the Braves were 8–22; they suffered yet another loss. Critics said he was making a mockery of the game.

If you were League President Chub Feeney, would you do anything about the rather awkward situation?

The Ruling: Feeney scoured the rule books and found a little-known clause that prohibits a manager from being involved in the ownership of his team. Needless to say, Feeney was quick to quote the rule and bar Turner from future dugout dealings.

Chapter Seven

UNLIMITED POWER

According to most baseball sources, one commissioner more than any other had autonomy. That man with the unlimited, unquestioned power was the first commissioner of the game, the legendary Judge Kenesaw Mountain Landis. He reigned with an iron hand and, at times, with unfair inconsistencies from 1920 until his death 24 years later.

In this chapter, you're given Landis-like power. In real life, the days of such power are gone. Decisions are often disputed by (or require approval by) powerful groups such as the Players' Association. But don't worry about it—*you* answer to no one.

Start by considering some concerns of baseball people who were surveyed in 1999. They were asked what, if anything, about the game they would change if they could. See if you agree with them and would implement their changes, or if you'd stick with the status quo.

First Issue

Joe Nossek feels the offense is getting out of hand in today's game. His change, he said, is, "I'd give the pitchers a little bit of an edge by raising the mounds now. The hitters are getting so big and strong, the pitchers are falling behind a little. He cited the seemingly infinite amount of home runs being hit of late. He believes the "offense and defense need to be equalized."

In 1968, with pitching so dominant, baseball decided to handicap the pitchers. Beginning the following year the mound was lowered from 15 inches to the currently required 10 inches. In 1968, dubbed "The Year of the Pitcher," the average E.R.A. in the American League was a minuscule 2.98. The National League's E.R.A. was almost identical at 2.99.

Compared to now, those numbers are insane. For example,

in 1999, only about six pitchers had an E.R.A. in the 3.00 neighborhood; in 1968 that was the E.R.A. for an ordinary, average pitcher. The greats had numbers like: 1.60 for Luis Tiant; 1.81 by Sam McDowell; 1.95 turned in by Dave McNally; Denny McLain (who won 31 games) had an E.R.A. of 1.96; and Tommy John was also under 2.00 at 1.98. The National League had two men below 2.00—Bob Bolin at 1.99 and Bob Gibson with his incredible 1.12. To this day, that ranks #4 on the all-time modern day list. Gibson was as stingy with runs as Silas Marner was with his precious gold.

After the mound was lowered, E.R.A.s were raised. In the Senior Circuit the average skyrocketed to 3.60, up by over 20%. In the American League the increase was almost identical (to 3.63). Overall, batting averages soared 16 points higher. Thus, in one swoop, a solid .284 batter became a glittering .300 hitter.

Now, all this gets back to Nossek. He thinks going back to 15-inch mounds is too drastic. First of all, he concedes, "I kinda think there might be a few mounds around a little higher than 10 inches right now." Still, he would allow all the ballparks to nudge the mound up a bit.

Nossek also said umpires aren't too strict in enforcing the height rule, but if you had the power, you could raise the mound and make the umps crack down on violators.

Rick Helling, a 20-game winner for Texas in 1998, observed, "Baseball has been a very cyclical sport as far as offense has dominated, then defense and pitching, then offense again. I think you need to get it somewhere in the middle where you have eras where it's very even. Right now we're in a very offensive period. In the 70's and 60's it was very pitching-oriented, it goes back through history like that—every 10 or 15 years or so it seems to switch. You'd think you'd be able to figure out something to where it would be a more even type of game."

So, here's your first decision. Help the pitchers, or keep the game as is? Can you figure a way to even things out? You're on your own here, as there seems to be no simple solution. Who knows, maybe the Nossek solution would help, or maybe you want to keep the game as explosive as it's been of late.

Listen When Billy Williams Speaks

At first thought, Billy Williams said, "I wouldn't change anything about the game because it's a great game." After a pause, he mentioned a problem with the designated hitter rule: "I would change that to simply make the game the same [in both leagues by dropping the D.H. rule]. If you've been the designated hitter in the minor leagues, and you get to the major leagues and continue doing it, I think you consider yourself half of a ballplayer. We don't see the guys that might work a little bit more to make themselves a better outfielder or infielder." He says they often feel, or act, like they're locked into the D.H. role.

So, he said, "I would get rid of the D.H. because I want the game to be the same in the American League and the National League so nobody will get hurt [be at a disadvantage] during the World Series or crucial [interleague] games."

Williams feels this way despite the fact that, as he observed, "I was a D.H. out in Oakland, but baseball has done a good job in the past staying with what they had. It's a traditional game, and I'd like to keep it that way."

What would your verdict be on the D.H. issue?

Consider Other Viewpoints

Before deciding, consider what third baseman Todd Zeile said: "I'm not a big fan of the D.H. I don't think that the old adage that it creates jobs is true. Somebody's hiding behind that rule because what you're really doing is taking a job away from a younger kid. There are still 25 guys on a club; the D.H. isn't adding a person.

"It's just prolonging somebody's career who, in most circles, has had a good successful career and been able to do a lot of things in the game. He may be keeping that 25th guy off the roster who might have a chance to at least make a living at this game," concluded Zeile.

Helling looks at the D.H. debate a bit differently. "The

D.H. situation is something you could look at; either doing away with it, or having it in both leagues. I know a lot of purists think it's neat to have two separate leagues, but the argument there, too, is if you do away with it, you're going to lose some great players like Edgar Martinez or a Paul Molitor when his career was coming to an end.

"To me, if you're that good of a hitter, they'll find a place for you to play. You can play first base, it's not that hard to play first base. You look at a lot of the great hitters in the National League, as their careers went on, they ended up playing first base because there's no D.H. there. I don't think there's any question Martinez, or Molitor, or Harold Baines could play first if they had to; they just don't have to, so the D.H. is a luxury."

Hard-throwing pitcher Steve Karsay had more ammunition against the D.H. He likes the aspect of National League play, sans D.H., where "the pitcher gets up there and stays in the game and hits. Sometimes he depends on himself to get a bunt down to keep himself in the game. I think it's just the fundamentals of baseball that if you can have the pitchers do the things the other guys are doing, be an all-around player, it makes you a better athlete."

Finally, the opinion of the 1984 National League Rookie of the Year and Cy Young Award winner from 1985. Dwight Gooden said, "I'd get rid of it, that's the one thing about the game I'd change."

Agree with Thome?

See if you agree with a drastic and innovative move that All Star Jim Thome came up with. "I'd change the minor league pension and give them more pension for certain years they played in the minor leagues—just like the major leagues. Maybe not [based on] ten years [as it is in the majors], but coordinate it where the minor leaguers would be taken care of."

Under Thome's system, even if a player never made it to the major leagues, he'd get some financial protection. Sounds fair.

Realignment?

Rick Helling feels baseball does need a more logical geographical realignment than the current configuration of teams. Sure, Milwaukee moved to the National League in the 1990s, but do you agree with Helling?

His argument, especially since he pitched for Texas, which was in the Western Division along with distant West Coast teams such as Anaheim, Oakland, and Seattle, was simple: "It just doesn't make any sense for us to be in the Western Division. The three other teams in our division are two hours behind us [due to the time zones].

"I think realignment is important, especially setting up some geographical rivalries. I mean, we don't even play Houston, and we don't play St. Louis. And those are two of the closest teams to us; we've never played them."

View from the Minors

Paul Carey, the 1999 manager of the minor league Savannah Sand Gnats of Class A, has a pet peeve. If he were the commissioner, there's one rule he'd get rid of in a heartbeat.

"I don't like the rule about charging the mound from the pitcher's point of view," he said. "There's nothing he can do— he's gotta be able to defend himself, but if he does, he's tossed.

"Umpires came to us in spring training and went over rules. All a pitcher can do in a situation where a batter charges is try to tackle the attacker." Carey said this is the official viewpoint at all levels, and it's unfair.

It's also unfair in that, as Carey said, "It seems like you can't even pitch it inside, but we tell our pitchers to throw inside— don't be afraid. You have to throw inside. If you miss inside five or six inches, you may hit them, but you're not a head-hunter." Yet, not all pitchers in baseball will listen to such instruction, as they may fear retaliation by batters all too willing to charge the mound.

As a side note, the charging of the mound gets to be ludicrous at times. One major league pitcher had a potentially perfect game broken up late in that contest when he hit a batter. Instead of realizing that hitting him was the last thing in the world the pitcher wanted to do, the batter became outraged and started out towards the mound as if he was, as they say in the fight game, "ready to rumble."

All things considered, could you come up with a better system than currently used, concerning players' charging the mound?

Padding

If you were the commissioner, would you address the current situation in which many players are wearing so much padding they resemble a police dog trainer in a K-9 unit? Men such as Mo Vaughn, Craig Biggio, Jeff Bagwell, David Justice, Brady Anderson, and many others simply have no fear of being hit by a pitch. They lean way out over the plate figuring if they get jammed and hit, so what, it ain't gonna hurt.

Biggio, who is about as tough as they come, says he began wearing the padding in 1996 to protect his left elbow, which had been drilled twice over a three-day span. By late 1999 Biggio owned the distinction of having been hit by more pitches than any active player.

He stated that while he didn't mind aggressive pitchers who throw inside, he wasn't about to act macho, get hurt, then hurt his team even more by having to sit out games due to injury. Why allow a pitcher to hit his elbow and try to intimidate him, he wondered. He even stated he planned on wearing the padding indefinitely.

On the other side of the coin, two big-name pitchers, Orel Hershiser and Tom Glavine, have publicly expressed concern over players' wearing such gear.

Would you let men such as Biggio wear the protection? Here are some rulings you could consider. Men wearing such "armor" would not be permitted to go to first base when hit by a pitch that strikes their padding. You could also simply ban all such pads. Then again, you might maintain the way things are now.

Are Games Too Long?

Years ago, baseball games could be played in around two to two-and-a-half hours. Games under two hours weren't considered freakish. Nowadays, three- to three-and-a-half–hour contests are seemingly becoming the norm. Game Five of the 1999 N.L.C.S. between the Mets and Braves went 15 innings and approached the six-hour mark. The two seasons that have produced the longest average time for nine-inning games are 1994 and 1999. In 1994 that average time was 2 hours and 54 minutes; the 1999 average was just one minute short of that length.

Do you think games are too long? If so, you might agree with sensational shortstop Omar Vizquel's suggestion. "If I had the power," he said, "I'd probably shorten the game to seven innings instead of nine." He said he'd simply want to make the games quicker. If his proposal did become a reality, statistics and records would no longer have the meaning they have had for decades, but everyone's entitled to his or her opinion.

Vizquel also jokingly said he'd "bring the fences in, make them shorter so I could hit a lot more home runs since I'm not a home-run hitter."

Is the Season Too Long?

Do you feel the 162-game schedule is too long? At one time the season ran 154 games. Would you change the length of the season? All Star Rafael Palmeiro would. He said, "I would shorten the season to about 140 games."

Ban the Trades

Shortstop Royce Clayton has an unusual plan. If he were the commissioner of baseball, he would not allow young players to be traded. "People don't really understand the effects of a trade," he began. "There can be animosity when a player leaves. Trades can sometimes hurt a player. Some guys are absolutely devastated by some trades. They've been in a city for a long time, have their families established, and developed a close relationship [with the city], and before you know it, one day you're gone.

"If it were at all possible, young talent would come up and not worry about being traded. I think it would be good for the fans, too, to have a player locked up for a long time. I'd say for about six years. You'd have more stability and the chance for the fans to get to know the player," concluded Clayton.

Chapter Eight

THE COMMISH
—'99 VERSION

In this chapter you again are given the power to make the decisions a commissioner or league president must make. This time, though, each of the following scenarios is an actual case taken from the files of 1999. First, though, a few thoughts by current players on the power of the commissioner and league presidents.

Opinions

John Smiley, a one-time 20-game winner, offered his opinion: "I think they're pretty fair; they're not as bad as the N.B.A. Some of those $10,000 fines in the N.B.A. are pretty steep. To take a guy out of the lineup for three or four days, or for a pitcher to miss a couple starts, that's pretty high [for a penalty]. And, if the team doesn't pay [a player's monetary fine], like the year Marge Schott, the Reds owner, didn't pay, the guys had to pay out of their own pocket."

He recalled a player's getting suspended without pay for three days in Cincinnati. Schott, unlike many owners, would not make up for the lost salary, and Smiley says that can be pretty tough, as "that's a lot of money for some guys." All in all, though, he felt the punishments were fair.

Brian Moehler, a right-handed pitcher, agrees. "I think they're pretty consistent, it doesn't seem like they vary too much from fine to fine. If you throw at someone on purpose or if you retaliate, the penalties are pretty standard."

Another pitcher, Rick Helling, agreed: "For the most part, they [the rulings] all have a precedent, and they [league presidents] take it back to somebody who did something similar, and you usually get about the same thing others did. For the most part, they're pretty consistent."

Surprisingly, one player, pitcher Scott Erickson, said fines and suspensions are "probably not hard enough sometimes." The Cleveland Indians are glad that's true at times. In August of 1999, after getting plunked by a pitch, David Justice not only charged the mound against Troy Percival of the Angels, he also threw his batting helmet at Percival.

Both combatants were issued a three-game suspension. While such a suspension is normal for an "assault" on the mound, throwing equipment could have stiffened the suspension. Manager Mike Hargrove of the Indians admitted, "I'm surprised it's only three, and very thankful."

Justice concurred, "I thought it would be a lot worse. I would prefer it be nothing, but I realize there's got to be some penalty. Three games is not bad."

Jesse Orosco, who has pitched in more games than any man in the history of the game, said he believes that, as a rule, "They make it the stiffest fine they can [for fighting] because they're trying to eliminate these things from happening.

"If you give guys just one day or two days [suspensions] or you don't fine them, stuff could happen again and trigger [more on-the-field problems]," said Orosco.

He did point out that, if a relief pitcher and a starting pitcher are suspended for, say, three days each, "it will hurt the reliever more." It's unavoidable, though, he said. "What are you going to do, you going to suspend a starter for 21 days? You could say he has to miss two starts, but you can't do that either because then you ruin the whole team because of the rotation [being out of sync then]."

I Beg to Differ

Tigers manager Larry Parrish sees it differently than Orosco: "You see that a lot of times where you're going to disagree with the ruling that comes down. To me, for instance, a starting pitcher, who throws at somebody which causes a fight, gets thrown out of the game and suspended for three days. Well, he doesn't pitch till the fifth day [his spot in the rotation], so this doesn't do anything to him. If a position player gets suspended for three days, that's three [missed] ball games.

"So, a starting pitcher should be suspended for three starts, not three games," he said. He added that even a relief pitcher suspended for three days might only miss, say, two games that he'd actually pitch in. "It effects an everyday player more than it does a pitcher, and that's not fair," he concluded.

Another Use for Sandpaper

It's interesting that Moehler thinks the rulings on suspensions are pretty fair, because Moehler himself was involved in a 1999 case. It began with him on the mound for Detroit during a game between the Tigers and the Tampa Bay Devil Rays on the first of May.

It was a tight contest (Detroit wound up losing, 4–3), which may have been part of the reason Moehler scuffed the baseball. He used some sandpaper, which he had concealed, to doctor the ball. Such balls can move up to an extra six inches, making it tough on the batters. The only problem was he got caught by veteran umpire Larry Barnett, who spied a small piece of sandpaper on Moehler's left thumb (not on his pitching hand).

Actually, the ump was responding to a complaint by the Devil Rays. A sharp-eyed Jose Canseco observed Moehler rubbing the ball into his left thumb.

Moehler's manager, Larry Parrish, said, "There's not a pitching staff that doesn't have a guy who defaces the ball." He may be correct; Moehler certainly wasn't the first (nor will he be the last) man to alter the surface of the ball. Men such as Gaylord Perry, Whitey Ford, Rick Honeycutt (with his thumbtack sticking through a Band Aid he had on his finger in 1980 with Seattle), and Joe Niekro come to mind.

Niekro was with the Minnesota Twins in 1987 when umpires accused him of throwing an illegal pitch that darted

erratically—as if his knuckleball wasn't bad enough. When the umps told him to empty his pockets, Niekro cupped an emery board in his hand and tried to drop it to the ground as he turned his pocket inside-out. His only problem, though, was he wasn't slick enough, and the board didn't fall inconspicuously—it flew out of the pocket, visible to the world.

Your only problem now is how you'd handle Moehler—exactly how stiff would your punishment be?

Real Life

Some people have gone so far as to suggest that the spitball be legalized. Since it hasn't been thrown legally since 1934, though, you must deal out a penalty to Moehler. In reality, the American League suspended him for 10 days.

By and large, if a player throws an illegal pitch or uses an illegal bat, he'll face seven to ten games of suspension. Albert Belle, for example, was suspended for ten games, but appealed the penalty and had it reduced to seven games. Chris Sabo was also caught with a corked bat in 1996 and missed seven games.

There are exceptions, of course, depending upon who is doling out the punishment, and other circumstances. Back in 1981, Dan Ford was suspended only three days for using an illegal bat.

Who Was That Masked Man?

On June 9, 1999, New York Mets Manager Bobby Valentine got into an argument with home-plate umpire Randy Marsh in the 12th inning. Marsh ruled that Mets catcher Mike Piazza was guilty of committing catcher's interference.

Valentine argued so long and so vociferously, he eventually was ejected from the game. Moments later, according to information that was officially reported to the National League, Valentine returned to the Mets dugout wearing glasses and sporting a false mustache. Senior Vice President of the National League Katy Feeney stated, "He was ejected and came back to the end of the dugout in a disguise."

Valentine was quoted as saying, "You don't know that was me. I tried to loosen up the team for just a minute." So, on one hand, he seemed to be saying it wasn't him, but then he seemingly admitted it was him by adding that the reason that he wore the disguise was to provide some levity.

Later he admitted he was the man of mystery, but added he never did go back into his team's dugout. "The picture looked like I was in the dugout, but they got it all wrong," Valentine contended. Sounds like a bad case of denial.

At any rate, the league decided to view a videotape of the Case of the Incognito Manager. Assuming you saw the tape and identified the masked man as Valentine, what punishment would you dish out?

What happened? National League President Leonard Coleman fined Valentine $5,000 and imposed on him a two-game suspension.

In addition, Valentine was subjected to some ridicule for

his antics. Steve Lyons, a television commentator, realizing some of the Mets players weren't too enthralled with their manager, made this comment: "This will be the only suspension where the players actually lobbied to have the suspension lengthened." A sportswriter felt the disguise wasn't all that unusual in that "Valentine has been masquerading as a major league manager for years." In fairness, Valentine did lead his Mets into post-season play in '99.

Foreign Substance

A 20-year-old relief pitcher for the Arizona Diamondbacks by the name of Byung-Hyun Kim got into a bizarre jam in 1999 as well. He was pitching on June 9th, in just his sixth game in the majors, when a bandage with a gooey substance flew out from the sleeve of his uniform.

The Chicago Cubs first baseman, Mark Grace, was immediately suspicious, so he retrieved the bandage and took it to the umpires. They huddled for a moment, then decided to eject him from the game.

Kim claimed the substance was a heat balm that he wore to keep his shoulder loose. He said he hadn't planned on wearing it during the game, he'd just forgotten to take it off. He further asserted that he'd always used the balm when he pitched in his native country of Korea.

Arizona manager Buck Showalter came to Kim's defense, calling it an innocent mistake, saying that Kim didn't use the heat balm to gain any advantage. After all, it wasn't as if he was using it to doctor the ball in the style of, say, a Gaylord Perry.

Now, consider two factors: first, the fact that the umpires did toss him from the game; and, second, his side of the story and the words of his manager. Would you suspend Kim for wearing the foreign substance?

The real decision: Five days after the incident the league ruled they would not suspend Kim. Still, like Valentine, Kim took some ribbing. Grace joked, "You have to give him credit. Most guys don't start cheating until later in their career."

T.V. Time: Leave It to Leonard

The next case involves Leonard Coleman, who was president of the National League in 1999. In June of that season, the Cardinals were playing the Marlins when controversy broke out with hurricane force. Florida's Cliff Floyd hit a ball that he felt struck the wall above the scoreboard at Pro Player Stadium, making it a home run. Umpire Greg Gibson said the ball actually hit the scoreboard and ruled Floyd had to stay put at second base.

Umpire crew chief Frank Pulli tried to settle the dispute by intervening; he ruled it was a home run, pulling the Marlins within one run of the Cardinals. Naturally, at that point, the St. Louis bench became apoplectic. Caught in the middle, and trying to get the call right, Pulli went to the dugout and gazed at replays on television cameras. There was no doubt, the ball hit short of the home run region. The final ruling cost Florida a run.

Floyd still felt cheated of a home run and raved that baseball, unlike football, has never used replays. Likewise, the Marlins, who played the game under protest, were angered because if Floyd had been given the homer, the strategy of the game would have become entirely different from how the game played out. A home run would've made the score 4–3. Eventually, the final score wound up being 5–2, with the Marlins losing.

If you were the commissioner, would you have upheld the Florida protest, causing the game to be replayed at a later meeting between the two teams? If so, the game, of course, would have been resumed at the 4–3 score and the batter due up after Floyd would be at the plate.

The outcome: Basically Coleman said the Marlins were correct in that there is no such thing as instant replay in baseball. Then he said, "However, it does not follow that the protest should be sustained." Protests, in fact, are rarely upheld. Unless an umpire blatantly blows a call based on the actual rules of the game (as opposed to a judgement call), protests are denied.

If you ruled in favor of replays, you're not alone. Many

experts feel that if the technology exists to get calls right, which is what Pulli was doing, then we should use that technology.

You versus Selig

During the Bud Selig era many changes have occurred in baseball. Again, there is no right or wrong answer per se, but which of the following concepts recently ushered onto the baseball scene would you support or eliminate?

- Interleague play: Most experts and players either love it or hate it.
- Three divisions instead of two (as had been the setup since 1969).
- The introduction of a wild-card team that is permitted to join division winners in playoff competition along the road to the World Series.
- Realignment of teams, including the move of the Milwaukee Brewers from the American to the National League.

A Few Thoughts on Innovations

Paul Carey, who was once in the Orioles system, said that if he could, "the first thing I'd do is go back to two divisions in each league. No, I'd go with two leagues, then the World Series." That's the way the game was played from the first decade of the 1900s up until 1969.

"You bust your butt for 162 games and win by, say, 25 games, then play a hot team or a team with two good, hot pitchers, and you lose," he observed.

Meanwhile, another "nay" vote on Selig-favored moves comes from manager (of Toronto in 1999) Jim Fregosi. "I'm an old-fashioned guy." he said. "There's 162 games. Why should we play for a wild card? The object is to win your division."

Part 4

YOU'RE THE UMPIRE

In this section, you're on the spot. Right down there on the field in front of the players, managers, TV cameras...and fans! How are your decision-making skills now?

Chapter Nine

KNOW YOUR RULE BOOK?

In this quick chapter, you'll be asked to test your knowledge of baseball's rule book. Some of the problems are easy ones, while others may, in fact, be deceptive. Either way, you make the call.

Oldie but Goodie

Here's a situation that's frequently talked about but rarely happens. A high pop-up follows a U.S. Army mortar-like trajectory. A bevy of infielders, including the pitcher, settle under the ball. Confusion concerning who is going to make the catch leads to the ball falling safely to the ground. As a matter of fact, it hits the mound on the third base side, and the slope of the mound causes the ball to carom into foul ground about halfway between home plate and third base. What's your call?

Answer: Since no fielder touched the ball in fair territory, the ball is treated the same as if it had been a slow roller that settled in foul territory. It's merely a foul ball. This play actually happened on August 7, 1999, when the Giants' J.T. Snow launched the pop-up. Several players converged on the ball, but second baseman Brett Boone called for the ball. When he was unable to make the play, the ball fell to earth, hitting the mound.

One report said the infielders looked like a bunch of Little Leaguers letting the ball drop. Still, some credit must go to shortstop Ozzie Guillen, who alertly turned a defensive blunder into a harmless foul ball. When he saw the path the ball began to take after hitting the mound, he let it go, waited until it crossed the foul line, then pounced on the ball, killing the play.

Out of the Baseline

Let's say speedy Roger Cedeno is on first base when a ground-ball is hit to second baseman Pokey Reese. The ball gets to Reese a split second before Cedeno does, so, using his quickness, Cedeno skirts around the fielder. He eludes Reese, semicircling around him, and Reese decides not to risk a throw to second for the force, going to first instead to retire the batter. Was Cedeno permitted to run around Reese? If so, how many feet out of the base path is Cedeno allowed as leeway?

Answer: Cedeno is allowed to avoid Reese, but only if he remains within three feet of the baseline.

Similar Scene

A runner is on first base when the ball is hit to the shortstop, who steps on second then guns to first for a double play. The runner off first is out the moment second base is touched on this force play. Let's say he sees he's out and freezes for a moment in the baseline.

Then, seeing the throw to first is nearly on a collision course with his body, the runner moves into the ball. When the ball hits him, the batter is able to beat the rap and the double play is averted.

What would the rule book say about this play? Is it legal? Did the runner violate a rule when the throw hit him?

Answer: As the play is described here, the umpire should have called a double play since the runner deliberately moved into the throw. It is, though, a judgement call.

This very play happened during the fourth game of the 1978 World Series. Lou Piniella of the Yankees was at the plate with Thurman Munson on at second and another man on first. If you're a trivia whiz, you may recall the runner, who jutted his hip into the flight of the ball, was Reggie Jackson. The shortstop who made the throw after getting the force out at second was Bill Russell of the Los Angeles Dodgers. In that case, the umpires did not feel Jackson intentionally interfered with the throw.

That controversy took place in the sixth inning with New York down by a 3–0 score. The umpire's call helped the Yankees rally as Munson scored on the play and Piniella ended up on second base instead of being ruled out. Eventually, they scored two in that sixth inning, and went on to win, 4–3. They went on to take the World Championship in six games.

Can an Ump Interfere?

Imagine Tony Womack is on first base when he gets the steal sign. Catcher Charles Johnson quickly comes out of his crouch and is about to rifle the ball to second, trying to nab a would-be base-stealer. The home-plate umpire inadvertently gets in Johnson's way, though, and actually bumps his arm. The ball sails wildly into centerfield and the runner advances to third. What's your call?

The rule book reveals: In this situation, the ball is dead due to the umpire's interference (it doesn't matter that his bump was unintentional). The runner must return to first base.

Incidentally, if Johnson were able to throw out the runner despite the interference, the umpire's contact would be ignored and the out would be recorded.

Appealing Play

Let's say it's the ninth inning of the All-Star game of 2001. Put Craig Biggio on first base and Tony Gwynn on second with two men out in a tie contest. Jeff Bagwell then singles sharply to center field where Ken Griffey, Jr., comes up with the ball. Both runners were off at the crack of the bat, so they each advance two bases. That means Biggio scored the winning run for the host National Leaguers. But wait, further imagine that Gwynn missed second base. This blunder makes things interesting. If the defense spotted the infraction and appealed at second base, what ruling would you make?

Answer: Because Gwynn never touched second, a base he had to reach since Bagwell's hit forced Gwynn to advance, a force play is still in effect. Therefore, by appealing at second, Gwynn's out becomes a force-out. The rules state no run can score if the third out is a force-out. Time for extra innings.

You can tell this is an imaginary situation because Gwynn is far too smart to make such a mistake. He probably wouldn't have even tried for third base since his run meant nothing.

A Tie Goes...

Kenny Lofton hits a Baltimore chop off the plate. The opposing shortstop, Alex Rodriguez, charges the ball, takes it bare-handed, and laser-beams the ball to first. Lofton and the ball arrive at the same time, a photo finish. An old rule that every child who ever played sandlot baseball knows is this: A tie goes to the runner.

Your questions: Is this an unwritten rule or is it a bona fide one? Is this concept of a runner's getting close plays fact or fallacy?

Answer: It is an unwritten rule. Further, it is a rule that kids might use playing in a backyard somewhere, but it is not a major league rule. At the big league level, the assumption is that there are no ties. A runner is either out or safe depending solely on the call of the ump; Lofton either beat the throw by a nanosecond, or he's out.

Strange Hit-and-Run Call

An absolutely crazy play involving Jay Bell and Kirk Gibson took place in the 1990s when they were with Pittsburgh. A fellow Pirate, Coach Milt May, put it this way: "We had something happen, it was the only time I've ever seen it, when Gibson was off first base and Bell hit a groundball in the hole on a hit-and-run, and the hole was wide open. Gibson ran so hard, his helmet fell off and the groundball hit in his helmet and stayed there.

"He thought it went into right field and was rounding second and going to third when the second baseman got the ball out of the helmet and threw him out at third. I mean that's something; how can that ever happen?!"

Bell's version was a bit different since he stated the ball hit the helmet and then ricocheted directly to the second baseman. Either way, it was certainly a bizarre play, but is the ball still live or should you call for a dead ball? If the ball is dead, does the runner return to second?

The proper call: It's simple. The ball is live and the play stands the way it was.

Chapter Ten

SCENARIOS
AND
UMPS' VIEWS

In this chapter we first take a look at some real-life plays then hear from some umpires, getting their perspective on the game.

No-Hitter

On June 25, 1999, Jose Jimenez of the St. Louis Cardinals threw a 1–0 no-hitter against Randy Johnson and his Arizona Diamondbacks. With one out in the ninth inning, pinch hitter David Dellucci hit a sinking line drive off Jimenez. Right-fielder Eric Davis streaked in, dove, and made a backhand stab at the ball. Davis rolled over, then stood up, only to have the ball drop out of his glove. Was umpire Mark Wegner correct in saying this was a legal catch?

Answer: Yes, he was. It's the umpire's judgment, and replays did indicate Davis had the ball long enough. Technically, the rules say the release of the ball on a legal catch must be voluntary and intentional. Wegner must have felt (under Rule 2.00) that Davis had "complete control of the ball."

Still, umpires seemingly will give close calls to the defense if a player has just come up with a fielding gem, and/or if the defense is trying to preserve a no-hitter (both those situations were in effect for the Davis catch). Bang-bang plays at first are going to be called outs, for example.

Then there was the last out of the Don Larsen perfect game in the 1956 World Series. Many fans and experts alike believe the final strike on the final out of the game was actually outside the strike zone. Perhaps, but the fact remains that umpire Babe Pinelli rung up pinch hitter Dale Mitchell on a borderline 1-and-2 pitch. Interestingly, it was the last game Pinelli ever worked behind the plate in his career, since he retired after the '56 Series.

Classic Blunder

Speaking of post-season play, here's a memorable play from Game 1 of the 1996 American League Championship Series between the Baltimore Orioles and the New York Yankees. With Baltimore up by one run at 4–3 in the bottom of the eighth, Derek Jeter drilled the ball to right field. It appeared that the ball had just enough oomph to carry it into the stands for a homer. Still, the Orioles' outfielder, Tony Tarasco, was camped under the ball; clearly, he felt he had a chance at making the catch. Suddenly, a 12-year-old fan snared the ball, and the umpire, Rich Garcia, had to make the call. What should his ruling be?

What happened? The rule states that if the ball is over the fence, and a fan touches it, the hitter gets his home run. If a fan reaches over the field and touches the ball, forget the home run, it's fan interference.

Now, what really happened was Garcia perceived the ball was already into the stands, over the wall, so he gave Jeter the homer, tying the game. However, replays showed he had blown the call. In fact, Garcia himself, upon seeing the replays, admitted he had been wrong. That didn't placate the seething Orioles, especially since the Yankees went on to win the opener 5–4 in 11 innings. For the record, the O's did rebound to take the second game, but were then swept over the last three games, and the Yankees went on to win the World Series.

Is It Interference?

Another famous play in the League Championship Series came in 1998. The Yankees again were the host team, this time facing the Cleveland Indians in Game 2. The twelfth inning rolled around and the teams were deadlocked at one run apiece.

Cleveland had Enrique Wilson on first base when Travis Fryman laid down a sacrifice bunt to move the potential winning run into scoring position. The Yankees' first baseman, Tino Martinez, gloved the ball and threw for second baseman Chuck Knoblauch, covering first on the play.

Fryman, meanwhile, was running inside the first-base foul line, not inside the three-foot lane that runs the last 45 feet from home to first in foul ground. Runners are required to be within that path on plays like this one.

When the Martinez throw ricocheted off Fryman and rolled away, Knoblauch was livid. He felt the ump, who called Fryman safe, should have instead ruled he was out for interference. You might recall that Knoblauch's argument was so heated, he actually forgot to chase down the ball. This allowed

Wilson to romp around the bases and score, and Fryman to put down anchor at third base.

Now, your challenge is this: is a runner automatically out when struck by a ball in such a scenario?

By the rule book: According to the rules, he is not automatically out because he wasn't running in the proper lane; it's a judgment call. Some experts say Fryman didn't interfere because he actually beat the ball to the bag. In other words, he was already safe when the ball struck him, so he had a right to be where he was at that moment.

Two things remain certain on that play: 1) it was a tough call and 2) Knoblauch should have hustled first and asked questions later (something he readily admitted to after the game).

Minor League Umps

It's interesting to get the thoughts of minor league umpires in that the game they call is a bit different from the way the game is called at the big league level. Class A umpires, for example, work a two-man (not a four-man) crew. This presents unique problems.

Tyler Bolick and Ed Rogers, a 1999 umpiring team of the South Atlantic League, pointed out some difficulties. "The toughest play for us," said Bolick, "is the check swing with the umpire's position being from the middle." He was referring to the fact that in the majors a check-swing appeal ruling is made by an umpire on first or third, gazing at a good angle towards the hitter. With a two-man crew, the umpire in the field doesn't have such an angle.

Rogers said it's tough when the pitched ball hits a player's hands with the hands "not being part of the bat." He said, "The sound of hands being hit can sound like wood, and you say, 'What'd it hit?'" Plus, of course, he must make the call immediately.

He also feels a "home run with fans reaching over the fence, fan interference" is a challenge. Rich Garcia would certainly agree.

Bolick added yet another demanding play, "The steal of home. You gotta call the pitch, possible interference by the catcher or batter, a balk if the pitcher speeds up his motion, and if the runner is safe or out."

That's truly a tough one at any level.

Bumping

If a player makes contact with an umpire during the course of a dispute, must the umpire eject the player according to the rule book?

Everyone knows there are certain actions that will get a player or manager ejected at the drop of a hat. Just ask Earl Weaver, who dropped—actually, threw—many hats to the dirt in disgust, only to be promptly kicked out of the game. Umpires, though, can overlook some infractions.

Rogers said, "In the heated argument, contact will be made, but if a bump is willful and deliberate, contact definitely will not be tolerated—he'll be ejected immediately."

His partner, Tyler, elaborated, "Sometimes contact occurs and it isn't considered a bump, so we don't report it. Each case [that is reported] is an individual one that the league president decides."

Reactions to 1999 Umpire Suspension

Speaking of bumps, in 1999 umpire Tom Hallion was suspended for three games by N.L. President Coleman for bumping a player during an on-the-field dispute. Reactions to this reportedly unprecedented event varied. Paul Carey said he was definitely surprised, "but if you're going to suspend players, managers, and coaches for bumping, they have to be consistent. Umpires have to be accountable.

"When you're yelling, you're so close, you're bound to bump—you're in each other's face. And, now, with TV covering every play, such an incident might have blown over before, but now…" Carey's voice trailed off as he knew he had made his point. He believes baseball had to dish up some punishment due to Hallion's behavior.

In the meantime, Robert Williams, who played in the Negro Leagues, said the suspension surprised him, because "umpires are supposed to take charge [not incite things]. They seem now like they want to argue with players."

On the other hand, another Negro League player, Norman Lumpkin, stated, "I'm not surprised, it should've happened before. Some umps hold grudges—if you show them up, beware. They won't get even immediately, but they will get even with you."

INDEX

About the Author

Wayne Stewart was born and raised in Donora, Pennsylvania, a town that has produced several big league baseball players including Stan Musial and the father-son Griffeys.

Mr. Stewart now lives in Lorain, Ohio, married to Nancy (Panich) Stewart. They have two sons, Sean and Scott.

Mr. Stewart has covered the baseball world as a writer for nearly 25 years now. He has interviewed many Hall of Famers such as Nolan Ryan, Bob Gibson, Robin Yount, Gaylord Perry, Warren Spahn, and Willie Stargell.

He has written two other books for Sterling Publications, *Baseball Oddities* and *Baseball Bafflers*, to go along with the nearly-600 articles he wrote for national publications such as *Baseball Digest*, *USA Today/Baseball Weekly*, *Boys' Life*, and Beckett Publications. He has also written for many major league official team publications such as the Braves, Yankees, White Sox, Orioles, Padres, Twins, Phillies, Red Sox, A's, and Dodgers.

He has taught English in the Lorain City Schools for over 25 years and is currently teaching at Whittier Middle School.